BLACK SABBATH

CHRIS WELCH

BOBCAT BOOKS

London/New York/Sydney/Cologne

First published 1982 © Chris Welch & Proteus Books Ltd
This edition © 1988 Bobcat Books
(Bobcat Books is a division of Book Sales Limited)

Edited by Kay Rowley
Designed by Adrian Hodgkins

ISBN: 0.7119.1738.8
Order No: BOB 10120

All rights reserved. No part of this book may be reproduced in any form
or by any electronic or mechanical means including information storage
or retrieval systems without permission in writing from the publisher,
except by a reviewer who may quote brief passages.

Exclusive distributors:
Book Sales Limited
8/9 Frith Street
London W1V 5TZ, UK.

Music Sales Corporation
24 East 22nd Street
New York, NY 10010, USA.

Music Sales Pty Ltd
120 Rothschild Avenue
Rosebery, NSW 2018, Australia.

To the Music Trade only:
Music Sales Ltd
8/9 Frith Street
London W1V 5TZ.

Typeset by 5X Composing Ltd
Printed and bound in Great Britain by The Eagle Press,
Blantyre, Glasgow.

Black and white photo credits:
Jim Bryant: page 8, 11-15, 17, 36; Fin Costello: 77, 82/3, 88/9; Andre
Csillag: 18/9, 22, 24, 25, 27, 30, 34/5, 38; Robert Ellis: 2/3, 36, 37,
42, 48, 51, 54, 56, 58, 61, 62-64, 66/7, 68/9; Robert Ellis/Ross Halfin:
72, 74, 78/9, 93; James Fraser: 6/7, 9; Andrew Kent/LFI: 70/1; LFI; 40;
Denis O'Regan: 45; Barry Plummer: 1, 44; Neal Preston: 47;
Syndication International: 61.
Colour photos: George Bodnar, Jim Bryant, Robert Ellis, L.F.I., Denis
O'Regan and Barry Plummer.
Scrapbook material on pages 21, 29, 31, 52 courtesy of Kate Styles.

ACKNOWLEDGEMENTS
The Author wishes to thank the following for their help and co-operation.
John Grandison of the Black Sabbath Fan Club, Malcolm Dome of Metal
Mania, Brian Harrigan of the MM, Jim Simpson of Big Bear Records,
Norman Divall of Phonogram, Patsy at Jet Records, Chris Hussey, Harry
Shapiro and Kim for rare archive material, Marilyne for endless coffee,
typing and corrections and Kay for patience and Indonesian cuisine.

CONTENTS

Chapter 1:	COME TO THE SABBATH	6
Chapter 2:	PURPLE PIGS MIGHT FLY	12
Chapter 3:	A TOUCH OF VERTIGO	20
Chapter 4:	BLACK MISCHIEF	30
Chapter 5:	BATH TIME WITH SABBATH	46
Chapter 6:	LET SLIP THE PIGS OF WAR	56
Chapter 7:	MUSICALLY SPEAKING – SABBATH	68
Chapter 8:	NEVER SAY DIE	78
Chapter 9:	OZZY, BLOODY OZZY	86
Chapter 10:	BORN AGAIN	92
	DISCOGRAPHY	93

CHAPTER 1
COME TO THE SABBATH

Rain hisses and gurgles, church bells toll, thunder rolls around a black and forbidding sky. And then hark! – the most diabolical, hellish and infernal noise known to mankind – the sound of amplified, electric music.

A lone human voice, tortured, angry and full of menace utters a lycanthropic howl that must conjure Diabolus, the Evil One, Old Horny himself. 'What is this that stands before me?' cries our hero. 'Figure in black which points at me. Turn round quick and start to run. Find out I'm the chosen one . . . oh no!'

And look, there in the graveyard, a black shape with eyes of fire. All around him flames crackle and there is no escaping the wrath to come. 'Please, God help me!' moans the victim in terror.

A crashing of drums and guitars beat like the hammers of hell, and we stumble away from the scene, both shaken and stirred by the most dramatic vision e'er raised in rock. We have just witnessed the birth of Black Sabbath.

We whirl forward in time, to a vast auditorium in Akron, Ohio. Some 54,000 souls are packed into the hall and they growing increasingly impatient at the delay to the start of the show. Other groups have come and gone, and the bulk of the fans wants to see one band – Black Sabbath. But a key member of the band, their lead singer 'Ozzy' Osbourne is still far away from the stage, separated from his audience by a labyrinth of corridors and firmly ensconsed in his dressing room. There is a whisper of fear backstage tonight, unspoken amongst the roadies and security men and the promoter's staff. That audience is about to blow at any minute. They are fused, primed and ready to explode and should not be kept waiting another minute.

Ozzy eventually makes his way towards the stage with the rest of the group and peers out from the sidelines. Out there in the vastness of the auditorium are their American fans, thousands of them. Dedicated. Fanatical. Just like their English counterparts and indeed like Sabbath fans all over the world. Some are getting crushed up against the barriers and there could be injuries, missiles thrown, maybe a full scale riot. Just a few more seconds . . . and then with a crash of drums and guitars, the band take up firing positions and Ozzy, the supreme manipulator of audiences is out in front of them, arms outstretched

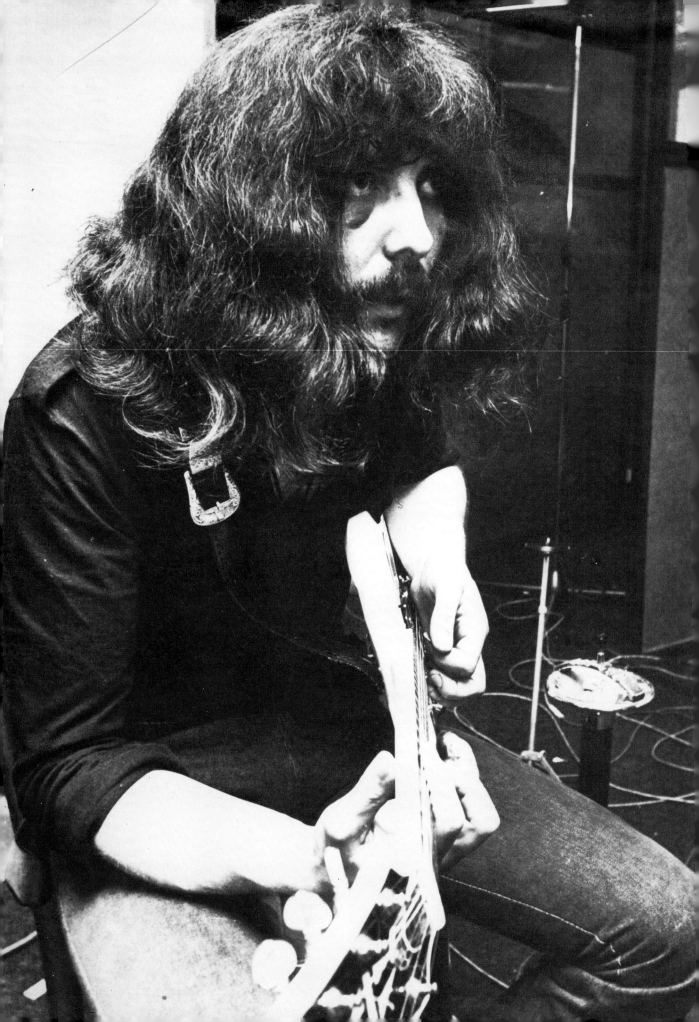

and two fingers raised in a peace sign that has somehow become a Black Sabbath signal of communication and brotherhood. The backstage folk allow themselves a sigh of relief for they have implicit trust in Oz. He knows exactly how to gauge an audience and how far he can push and arouse them. 'Give it five' he'll say sometimes, a smile creasing a sensuous mouth, fringed by long hair cascading in waves over his shoulders. Five more minutes of tension building before the band launch into a performance that has aroused fear and hostility from their critics and a loyalty and devotion from fans.

It is a polarity that has made Black Sabbath unique. They are a real people's band and it is the people who have carried them from obscurity and poverty in the clubs of Hamburg and Birmingham to a commanding position as one of the most successful – and uncompromising – bands in rock history.

The audience at Akron in the early Seventies reacted to a combination of sonic assault and battery, not by fleeing the consequences, which could be anything from crushed limbs to premature deafness but by embracing the four horsemen of the rock apocalypse as saviours and leaders on a wild ride to oblivion and ecstasy.

Black Sabbath then and now, represent everything that the rock establishment rejected. During the Sixties rock had become inextricably involved with a kind of liberal American peace and love movement that embraced everything from diet to politics. The idea of a youth movement devoted to peace in Vietnam, free love and rock music was attractive, worthy and at times a little sanctimonious. It left many people cold, particularly working class youth who could not identify with this esoteric concern for higher things, when they were still more worried about getting a job, a fast car and a girlfriend. Brown rice, yoga, the drug culture, and the rapidly increasing complexity of music, tended to isolate a large section of the potential audience for rock.

It is easy enough to define this trend with the benefit of hindsight but at the time, as the Sixties drew to a close, Black Sabbath with their direct appeal to mass audiences, seemed to represent a backward step, a wilful anomaly in an otherwise uniform march towards sophistication and progress.

And, of course, that is exactly what they were and remain a band who could claw back rock music's power to shock and dismay. Frank Zappa once said 'I just want to be comfortable,' when asked about the need for revolutions. Black Sabbath's triumph was to stop rock music ever becoming merely a comfort. They looked it squarely in the eyes, chewed off its head and spat out the pips of pretention.

But it was a mistake made by many to think that Black Sabbath simply represented all that was mindless and bad. This was a dismissive argument that lacked foundation and was born of prejudice. Yet set against a background of contemporary bands emerging at the same time as Sabbath, like Led Zeppelin, Yes, Jethro Tull and ELP, the confusion and dismay the lads from Aston aroused was understandable. Critics and many an earnest rock fan had been led to expect a steady kind of growth from the simplicity of the Sixties R&B movement. They were still debating the significance of the Beatles' *Sgt. Pepper* album when the church bells tolled and announced the arrival Black Sabbath's first album released on Vertigo in February 1970.

But for every aesthete quivering over the nuances of Ian Anderson's flute playing, there was a long haired youth in loon pants and denim jacket ready to prostrate himself in the front rows at the overwhelming, mind boggling, thunderous roar of this strange new band. Here was a tougher image than was presented by the well-meaning hippies, much more in keeping with the concrete jungle. This was music that seemed to reverberate off the sides of high rise developments, that vibrated like a fleet of container lorries cracking up the spaghetti junctions of the brave new planners' world. This was a suitable accompaniment to the sound of British cities like Birmingham, falling under the attack of pneumatic drills and being refashioned into echoing, crime-ridden rat runs.

There had been loud bands before. The Who, Jimi Hendrix and even those legendary pioneers the Yardbirds had all been capable of blasting ear drums and utilising the increasing power of amplification which tried to keep pace with the growing size of audiences. But here was volume used with a brutal violence that disregarded all previous ideas about restraint. There were no apologies. Black Sabbath were loud, hideously so and if you didn't like it, you could vacate the premises. Those who could take it were the chosen ones, initiates who had survived a ceremony made all the more impressive by its dabblings in sorcery and black magic.

It was a dangerous mixture to unleash on the young and impressionable, and there were those who feared its consequences — and indeed there was one tragedy which had tenuous links with Sabbath music. But this tampering with the powers of darkness was not unique to the band. There was a very real wave of underground interest in the occult that had spread through the British music scene during the late Sixties, born out of frustration, exhaustion and bitterness. In a fiercely competitive scene, where the Beatles had set a pattern of success that far too many thought they could emulate, at least in part, there was bound to be resentment and feelings of inadequacy. These were not directed against the Beatles in particular but against a little understood world of manipulative agents, managers, record companies and press. The idea of a secret, hidden but powerful force that could be used to defeat these rampaging enemies was seductive and appealing.

Many musicians began to investigate and attempted to utilise these powers when they felt all their efforts to gain just rewards for their work had failed. From a simple study of Tarot cards and astrology to involvement with holy magick and the like was but a step away. It is easy, and probably sensible to scoff at such things, if one wants to preserve the balance of the mind. My own view is that Black Magic is probably a real and little understood force, instinctively feared, and for good reason.

This undercurrent of interest in the black arts was not widespread but real enough and eventually led to its use as a powerful image for publicity and more simply to create an identity. Black Widow were another band to sing and write about black magic, who emerged, as fate would have it, at exactly the same time that Earth, the blues band from Aston decided to change its name to Black Sabbath.

But there was never any doubt which was the stronger band and the albums they released *Black Sabbath* and *Black Widow* bear no comparison. Sabbath had been turned into a tough, writhing animal of a group by long hours of playing to uncaring audiences for poor money in miserable conditions. Once unleashed, there was no power to stop them and all competition soon faded away.

Musicologists tend to dub Sabbath as the original Heavy Metal group, a phrase from science fiction that seems peculiarly appropriate to the doom laden overtones of their music. Incidentally as I write these words, a huge black thundercloud, emitting shafts of lightning is passing over my head, accompanied by lashing hail and rain, and as I pondered the significance of Black Sabbath in bed last night, I was beset with dreams of demons and apparitions. Coincidence? Of course not.

We must not allow ourselves to be distracted, even by signs of displeasure from the heavens. It was the Americans who introduced the term 'heavy metal,' and in Britain the clarion cry was simply 'Heavy,' or if you had trouble with consonants, 'eavy. It was claimed that Sabbath had stripped rock down to its essentials, relying on heavy riffs, battering drums and screaming vocals. This indeed became the format for dozens more groups in successive waves, as the Seventies progressed into the next decade. But in truth the music of Sabbath bears little relation to other groups in the genre and there has been a subtlety in their recorded output often overlooked. *Black Sabbath* itself was and remains a masterpiece of dynamism, a performance heavy with pregnant silences and controlled outbursts.

The men who created their own style are today hailed as heroes, where once they were damned as rock'n'roll felons. It is our purpose to examine the

rise of Ozzy Osbourne (vocals), 'Geezer' Butler (bass), Tony Iommi (guitar) and Bill Ward (drums), and to search into the history and origins of their band. We shall chart their successes and failures and perhaps redress the balance of critical opinion.

The fans have never been anything less than faithful. Once during the early days of the band's history when they were still perhaps hoping for an encouraging review, Tony Iommi mournfully pronounced, 'Nobody likes us, except the public.'

But international success came surprisingly quickly once their credentials had been established. Their days as Earth were buried and forgotten as they hit with *Paranoid*, a single off their second album of the same name in 1970. They also enjoyed a succession of gold albums, which have passed into the hall of fame, starting with *Black Sabbath, Paranoid, Master Of Reality, Black Sabbath Volume 4*, and *Sabbath Bloody Sabbath*. Later albums included *Sabotage, Technical Ecstasy, Never Say Die, Heaven And Hell* and most recently, *Mob Rules*.

Their life was a blur of touring and recording, punctuated by personal and management crises, which have left them older and wiser in the Eighties, and bereft of the man many considered to be their greatest asset, the dynamic Ozzy.

But Black Sabbath are still a potent force in their revamped form and enjoying a revival of interest that has made them once again, one of the biggest drawing bands in the world. How they got there and how they survived makes a fascinating tale, as we shall see, come hail, thunder and the demons of hell.

CHAPTER 2
PURPLE PIGS MIGHT FLY

Any band that calls itself Polka Tulk risks being doomed to obscurity. And it didn't take a four-piece band from Aston, Birmingham long to come to that conclusion. They hastily changed their name to Earth – and still seemed doomed to the same fate.

The name game is of paramount importance and can mean the difference between hoots of derision and eager acceptance in the fickle world of rock. When a new band is struggling out of the quagmire of poverty and anonymity, their choice of name is enough to alienate or impress potential audiences, and more important, those vital cogs in the wheels of the music business, agents, managers, record executives and critics. There is no doubt Polka Tulk was not a name to inspire greatness, nor lead to paths of glory paved with gold, or platinum albums.

But the best stories have humble origins and the decidedly humble Polka Tulk eventually grew into a rock legend. The change to Earth seemed to suit the

prevailing mood of the late Sixties. The blues boom was dying and hippies still held sway. It was, however, a time of transition. Many of the older groups broke up as failed attempts to break into America, drugs, personality clashes and financial squabbles took their toll. At least this shake down opened the floodgates for a new breed of warriors, straining at the leash.

Some of the new supergroups would be formed by experienced 'name' musicians who had already been through the mill, men like Jeff Beck, Jimmy Page, Eric Clapton, Rod Stewart, Keith Emerson and Ritchie Blackmore. They had already tasted fame and learned from the hard grind on the road with bands that won plenty of fans and hit records but never made the money that was due to them — their destinies often controlled by maverick managers who saw them all as pop stars rather than musicians with minds of their own.

But other newer bands who would break through to audiences hungry for rock excitement were made up of untried musicians. Like the fans, their expectations had been aroused by the promise of now defunct bands like Cream and the Jimi Hendrix Experience. There was a vacuum that had to be filled despite the predictions of many that the rock boom must surely be over, that there was nothing more that could be done with guitars, drums and amplification.

Earth sounded like they might be a bunch of peace-loving macrobiotic freaks, dutifully chewing brown rice forty times a mouthful, practicing yoga on prayer mats and clad in gaily coloured loon pants and the best quality kaftans.

They may have dabbled with such fringe activities but these boys were from Birmingham, a city that produced musicians with guts and a down to earth approach to life. Smoking dope was regarded as pleasant an occupation in the nation's Second City as it was anywhere else in the country. But even when Birmingham stalwarts like Stevie Winwood went beads and bells with Traffic, the more twee aspects of the 'alternative society' failed to appeal to the likes of Ozzy Osbourne and his chums in Earth.

After all, Earth were a blues band and already had a macho image. There were rumours of criminal activities whilst on tour and infringements of the law in Carlisle had made it necessary for them to return to Birmingham post haste. If they couldn't get much work at home, at least they could go along to watch other groups playing at Henry's Blueshouse, situated at the Crown Hotel in Station Street.

Every Tuesday night they paid their four shillings and six old pence admission, saw the best of the local bluesmen and got to meet the 'faces' on the music business scene. Among the first hundred members to join the club were John Michael Osbourne, Anthony Frank Iommi, Terence Michael Butler and William Thomas Ward.

It was through their visits to the club that they got to meet the man who was to have a profound, if short lived influence on their lives, and was to ultimately help them in their battle to win fame and acceptance.

Jim Simpson was a jazz trumpeter and band leader who had branched out into running his own record label and management company. Jim also ran Henry's Blues house and, of course, he was an inveterate blues and jazz fan, as well as a connoisseur of fine imported Belgian beers. Simpson as a musician and businessman was running a crusade for Birmingham musicians. When he despaired of the national music press ever taking any notice of Midlands talent, he started his own irregular newspaper, Big Bear. He booked blues stars from America as well as home grown blues talent.

He was, without doubt, the man best placed to help an up and coming new group and Earth were only too pleased when he took some interest in them. Jim ran Henry's Blueshouse and when musicians and promoter began talking, neither of them realised it was to be the start of a wild ride to the top, that would ultimately end in a long drawn out battle.

When Jim met Earth he found a group assailled by doubts and lacking in confidence. They did not know whether they should continue trying to play music together and they wanted Jim's opinion — was it worthwhile carrying on?

After their minor scrape with the law on earlier forays they were reduced to playing £10 gigs at parties for friends. Their music was raw, loud but already had a strange kind of hold over those audiences they could scrape together. They needed constant reassurance — but Jim was convinced — they had something. Pleased to find sympathetic ears they often turned up at his house in the early hours of the morning after a gig. Hours were spent over food and drink provided by Jim, discussing their problems, which always seemed worse if the gig had gone badly.

And there was always the solace and pleasant occupation of talking about music in general and making fresh discoveries about jazz and the blues under Jim's guidance and with the aid of his vast record collection. Years later Simpson still treasures a demo record made by the band called 'For Jim.' It must be the only jazz session ever recorded by Black Sabbath and features Tony Iommi playing a passable approximation of the style of Wes Montgomery, with Bill Ward backing him up with bebop drums. Another demo from the period shows the band as consumate rock'n'rollers in the traditional sense, playing a superb version of *Blue Suede Shoes*. Here Ozzy is shown to be a master vocalist, with an instinctive feel for lyrics and a cheerful way of scatting his way through those words he couldn't quite remember.

This was a band rich in talent and humour but undoubtedly still seeking their direction. In the mythology of Sabbath it is often claimed that Bill Ward 'was a bit of a basic drummer' or that 'Sabbath couldn't really play which was why they turned up the volume.' These early examples of their flexibility showed that basically all four members were highly competent musicians.

But there was no point in this strange, uncertain and wary bunch, delving into the realms of jazz. It wasn't really their scene, and as for the blues, it had almost been done to death, at least as far as the British scene was concerned. What had begun at the start of the decade as a fresh, youthful appreciation of the American blues tradition that spawned a rich lode of talent, had degenerated into a cliché ridden routine. The riffs and licks that once seemed so exciting had become worn out, and audiences were beginning to cringe.

One band of satirists, the Liverpool Scene, summed it all up with their spoof *I've Got The John Mayall Can't Fail, Chicken Shack, Fleetwood Mac Blues*. But the shuffle beat and whining slide guitars of the electric blues would eventually be revived, reshaped and turned into the basis for Heavy Metal. And the band that did the most reshaping was of course — Black Sabbath.

The Midlands had already made a big contribution to the national rock scene by the time Sabbath was putting its toe in the water. The Spencer Davis Group, the Move and the Moody Blues all had their roots in the area and many were the individual artists to gain prominence, like Denny Laine, Robert Plant and guitarist Clem Clempson. Birmingham itself provided quite a few places to play. Apart from Henry's there was also Mother's Club which featured the more progressive bands like Traffic, Juicy Luicy and the Nice. And there was the Town Hall, which featured concerts by the bands that had really hit the big time.

A smaller scene than London perhaps but it was none the less important for the Sabbatarians to break into and prove their worth. Being a broke, unknown musician was no fun at all, especially when, as Jim Simpson seemed to think, 'they had got something.'

All four members of this erratic bunch were born in Aston, Birmingham's inner city. Tony was born on February 19, 1948, Geezer Butler on July 17, 1949, Ozzy Osbourne on December 3, 1948 and Bill Ward on May 5, 1948. Tony had Italian ancestry and went to Grammar school and was possibly even more intent upon advancement than his confederates.

Growing up in a fairly tough neighbourhood they learned how to take care of themselves on the street, and early privations helped forge a bond between them that was cemented by their love of music. Ozzy Osbourne used to delight in telling the story (probably apocryphal) 'There was one time when

Bill and me couldn't go out at the same time. Somehow we'd end up only having one pair of shoes between us and we had to take it in turns to go out.' By coincidence that is exactly the same story that Who manager Kit Lambert used to tell about the Merseys, a popular Sixties duo. It must have gone around among all the struggling musos of the period.

After leaving school early, all four went into a succession of unsatisfactory jobs with only music to keep them sane. Tony began to show flair as a guitarist and in 1967 when they were all unemployed, they decided to form a band. Parents helped find the money for the necessary drums, guitars and amplifiers and Geezer recalls them 'spending months rehearsing in this cellar in Birmingham.'

After their spell as Polka Tulk they switched to Earth and began to play the blues as best they could on the city's club and pub circuit. It all seemed like a lot more fun than a day job and said Ozzy: 'I never realised the strength of the band. We were just four ordinary losers . . . we just bummed around in an old Transit van, playing anywhere just to get a gig.'

Jim Simpson booked them as an interval band at Henry's, part of his policy of encouraging local talent. The first time they played the club instead of giving them the normal five pound fee, he gave them a Henry's tee shirt each, apparently at their request.

What were Earth like at that primeval gig? 'Loud, rough and a bit directionless,' remembers Simpson. 'They were a blues band but it was the end of the blues boom. The musicians then had started to stand around and stare at their feet and not play with the excitement and feeling of the black American bands. It was all very boring and people got scared of booking blues bands.'

Jim says it had got so bad that promoters who offered a booking would demand nervously: 'They're not a blues band are they?' Such groups had deteriorated so badly into sloppy apathy that they had started to empty the clubs. In such circumstances the future for Earth looked bleak, or perhaps one should say – black.

One of the last local blues bands to achieve any sort of recognition and lift itself out of the trough of prevailing mediocrity was Bakerloo Blues Band featuring Clem Clempson who went on to fame with Colosseum and Humble Pie. But Tony Iommi at this time, while developing rapidly as a guitarist, was unlikely to match Clem for fluency and provide any sort of competition for a while yet. There was no doubt Earth had to find itself a new direction. But whither?

'We only opened Henry's to give Bakerloo a chance to play because nobody else was booking blues bands then,' says Jim. 'And that's how we ran into Earth and found this deep undercurrent of blues interest in the city.' The new group quickly won itself a hard core of local fans and later, when they became Black Sabbath they were the only local band to sell-out at the old club.

Jim was delighted to see this progress. He too had known the heartbreaks of being in a band, having played trumpet with Locomotive, which he gave up to take over as manager. He added Bakerloo and Tea & Symphony to his stable of groups and it seemed a spot of empire building might not go amiss.

The Birmingham rock empire would be run from a suburban living room in Edgbaston where dreams of riches and glory were fuelled with copious draughts of fine ales. For a year or so, everything looked fine, and even Locomotive had a hit with *Rudi's In Love*.

At first Jim claims he met a great barrier of resistance to Black Sabbath when it came to visiting London in search of record contracts and press interviews. It was rather like earth scientists' attempts to make contact with civilisations on distant galaxies. But other scientists have warned 'When the space telephone rings, don't answer.' The same advice might have served Jim in good stead as he innocently proclaimed the virtues and potential of his new signing around the music business.

He says now that he gave away all publishing and recording rights to the new band 'absolutely free.' Jim dealt with Tony Hall Enterprises based in London and he recalls: 'In those days it was totally impossible to get anybody to travel further north than Watford and I'm sure they didn't believe me when I raved about Sabbath. They had heard the rough demos we cut and they couldn't see anything musical in them at all. These weren't blues or jazz demos, these were actually recordings of the song *Black Sabbath*. They were songs that would subsequently sell millions of copies. Nobody could see it.'

The memory of the way Sabbath was ignored still pains Jim Simpson twelve years later and his face contorts into a wince of chagrin and frustration.

'I really gave Tony Hall a hard time and said "if you take my other bands, then you must take this because I believe in them!" Eventually they took them on for production, but Jim still had to go to 14 record companies.

Eventually David Platz, who owned half of Tony Hall Enterprises, put up £400 to make an album and work started in a 4-track studio off London's Tottenham Court Road. Jim wasn't trusted to be the producer and Roger Bain was brought in to take charge of recording. Once this was completed Jim once again had to trek around the record companies trying to drum up interest.

Throughout this period Jim felt he had the trust and confidence of the band. 'They had originally come to me for help because I had so many things going. There were times when they nearly broke up and we had to battle to keep them together. Ozzy would come round to my place at 4 am completely distraught because the band was getting nowhere.'

Jim admits it was tough on them when there appeared to be no light at the end of the tunnel. But it was tough on all the groups of youngsters who had pinned their faith in rock'n'roll to give meaning and

direction to lives that might have simply ended up on the dole queue or worse. Sabbath suffered a lot of emotional problems that led to fights and conflicts right from the beginning.

To keep them working and to knock them into shape Jim got them gigs in Germany, and in particular at the famous Star Club in Hamburg, where the Beatles had once sweated night after night. It has been suggested that the band had already played abroad when Simpson took over management but Jim is insistent: 'No, they hadn't got anywhere when I found them. I got all the German stuff for them and some Swiss dates which really seemed to pull them together.'

The process of turning Earth into Sabbath was a curious business wrought in part by external influences and by their own stubborn, emotional tendencies.

Jim is convinced the musical changes started at record sessions that took place at his house in Deblen Drive. 'Basically we listened to jazz and blues related records. They discovered their riff music from artists like Jimmy Rushing!'

It would astonish earnest musicologists, particularly in America perhaps, to discover that the Count Basie Orchestra, swingers from Kansas City, had ever been an influence on Black Sabbath, hailed as the founders of Heavy Metal, from Birmingham, England.

But Jim Simpson is adamant that Tony, Geezer, Bill and Ozzy listened with some interest to his treasured albums by the pianist whose bands had been swinging the blues since the 1930s. And if this seems far fetched then one need look no further than the first chorus of Wicked World from the Black Sabbath LP which was eventually released in February 1970 on the Vertigo label.

It was a track that has puzzled fans because of its unexpected use of the 'sighing hi-hat', played by Bill Ward in the manner of Basie's drummer Jo Jones. Jim's explanation that he had been indoctrinating the young musicians with old Basie records seems quite plausible. 'I know there is no relationship between Sabbath and Basie in their music, but the repetitive riff idea came out of those record sessions. In fact their stage show at that time included covers of some Jimmy Rushing songs. They liked the riffs small jazz bands played and it started a trend within Sabbath.'

It was unlikely that Sabbath got much chance to try out their jazzy ideas on the Germans who packed the Star Club in the late Sixties. Music was a cheap commodity that could be imported from the pool of talent in England. Bands were given board and lodgings and it was their job to keep the customers satisfied, dancing, drinking and preferably, not fighting.

Said Ozzy later: 'It was hard all right. It wasn't only the amount of work you had to get through. When the Beatles were talking about five sets a night, they weren't joking. We used to go on and off that stage like jacks in a box. It just seemed to go on forever. I had the feeling that they didn't care what we were doing on stage as long as something was going on. If we stopped or anything they used to go mad!'

It could be a soul destroying experience for young musicians and Ozzy in particular was heart broken by the indifference of the stolid punters. 'They just tried to be as cool as they possibly could. We'd be belting away up there and, you know, like NOTHING from them!'

Tony Iommi also has bitter sweet memories of those pioneering days. 'The audiences used to entertain us rather than the other way round. We had to do so many sets every night we used to run out of things to play. I mean we didn't have an enormous list of songs we could do anyway but it wasn't too bad. After we had done three shows though, we began to run out of material. So we used to play songs over and over again or just make a terrible mess of something we never really knew how to play.

'We had to do so many shows every night we started doing longer solos – all of us. It got so bad we ended up devoting whole sets to solos. We got Bill to do a drum solo which must have lasted half an hour. I used to do complete sets on my own on guitar. There was one time when we even managed to get Geezer to do a whole set soloing on bass. I don't think anybody noticed to be honest.'

The band played away staring at the strange people who frequented the Star Club. Some of them were startling even in those pre-punk days. 'There were some weird looking blokes out there and some of the women – God,' says Tony, flinching at the memory. 'A lot of the time it was hard to tell who exactly was who.'

One night a man walked in while Sabbath were playing dressed in a smart suit. He seemed so normal and respectable that in midst of the usual *clientele* he stood out and the whole band noticed him straight away. 'We all had a feeling he was going to do something strange,' recalls Tony. 'We were just worried what it might be. We were all hoping he wasn't going to shoot the place up. We watched him warily and then he came out into the middle of the dance floor. We were looking at each other and looking at him and thinking "God, what's he going to do?" '

'We were a bit worried. Then suddenly he did a handstand right in the middle of the floor. All the money fell out of his pockets, his wallet, his comb, everything. But he just ignored everything. He stayed up on his hands for a while, then he came down and walked straight out of the door. He didn't pick up his stuff or brush himself down. No one in the place said a thing. I reckon we were the only ones who noticed.'

Another night Ozzy spotted a pot of purple paint lying around backstage. In between sets he dis-

appeared. The rest of the band took to the stage for the next performance, wondering where he had gone. At the last moment Ozzy burst onto the stage painted purple from head to toe.

Geezer, Tony and Bill were astonished and then collapsed with laughter. But despite such drastic measures to arouse a response from the club goers, the audience didn't bat an eyelid. They ignored the purple painted teenager prancing before them and Ozzy had to admit defeat. It took him hours to get the paint off.

Someone must have been impressed by their dedication however. The band were booked back to the Star Club five times and they set a house attendance record.

Later the band were to tour all over Germany and Switzerland as Jim Simpson signed them to management contracts and got them more work at home and abroad.

The 'knocking into shape' process continued and began to have an effect, but perhaps not one that was entirely welcomed or understand by fans of jazz, blues and most British rock music of the period. Apart from painting themselves purple, the band had

already began increasing the volume of their performance, an instinctive reaction when audiences a few yards away were rudely engrossed in their private conversations and taking no notice of the creative artistes giving every fibre of their being.

'It used to drive us mad,' said Bill Ward. 'To think, we were working so hard, playing our guts out, while all these guys were sitting around and chattering. So we turned up the volume louder and louder until it was impossible for anyone to have a conversation. That seemed to work.'

The whole of the British rock group movement was born out of R&B and blues bands tiring of their original format as immitators in search of authenticity. They soon began writing their own material, a practice adopted by every major group from the Who, the Yardbirds and the Kinks onwards. Once the ground work had been laid, the task of evolving their own music was begun and that's exactly what happened to Earth, with cataclysmic results.

They began writing their own material, and combining this step with their workaday origins and constant feelings of frustration and confusion, a revolutionary brew began to ferment. But there was democracy in the camp. Every song they wrote was credited simply to Black Sabbath. Each member took an even share of the composing royalties which was a sensible practice. It avoided the kind of ill-feeling that a lopsided division of the spoils had generated in bands like Cream, leading to their ultimate demise.

One of the first songs they wrote together was a sensational piece that was to shape the whole of their future career – a musical drama filled with a sense of evil and foreboding. It was called . . . Polka Tulk. ('Some mistake here? Ed). Hold fast . . . it was BLACK SABBATH. And once 'twas written, its influence reached out and touched the lives of countless people. The echoes of its impact are still with us.

CHAPTER 3
A TOUCH OF VERTIGO

If 'Black Sabbath' sounded like a revolution against prevailing musical trends in 1970, then that was the deliberate intention. Ozzy Osbourne was quite emphatic about it when he later described the birth of their most important song. 'It was a reaction against all that peace, love and happiness shit that was going around at the time. I mean, all that stuff was incredible. The hippies said: "The world is so beautiful man." You only had to look around to see how crappy it was. It was ridiculous listening to that stuff, let alone playing it, so we just wrote about the world the way it really was and how it affected us – and we felt better in ourselves because we were being really honest. We didn't want to go through any of that phoney bollocks. And it turned out that it was a really important song for the band.'

Well it certainly gave the band a new name, just in time. They discovered there was another band going the rounds, also called Earth and confusion was mounting, sometimes with ludicrous results. One night Geezer, Tony, Bill and Ozzy were booked for a dinner and dance – an engagement which should have gone to the other Earth. 'It was a bit strange actually,' says Tony Iommi. 'There were all these people in suits and nice evening dresses and they were sitting waiting for us to play the pop songs of the day and maybe a few waltzes and quicksteps. I mean... I would have done it if I could, but there was just no way we could do any of those songs.'

'So we just had to go on and do our usual heavy set. I think they were a bit astonished actually. I don't remember that they enjoyed it too much.'

Later, on a return trip to Germany they discovered the other Earth had released a single so that decided them finally to change their name to Black Sabbath. But there was another crucial factor in the switch.

Says Jim Simpson: 'Suddenly – Geezer discovered Dennis Wheatley and came up with these black magic lyrics.' Wheatley is the renowned author of many tales of the supernatural including the classic **The Devil Rides Out**. His books, and the films based on them, enjoyed a new vogue during the Sixties, which it must be said, the much maligned hippies with their interest in all manner of weird phenomenon had helped instigate.

But how serious was the group's involvement with the black arts? Jim is insistent. 'There was no sinister implications about their involvement. Geezer just read the book and was captivated by certain lines in it. Maybe he became more interested in black magic later but originally it was simply because he read one book by Dennis Wheatley. The group shied away from any real involvement in magic rites and at times they were a bit worried about just the thought of having a black magic stance.'

It was ironic that having changed their name from Earth to avoid confusion, that another group came along at the same time, called Black Widow, who were profoundly influenced by the occult, had a male witch as a patron and wrote pieces like *Come To The Sabbat*. Once again the Sabbs considered changing their name. 'But we had gone too far along the road by then,' says Jim. 'We thought we'd lose what image we had, as people were beginning to latch onto it.'

'But the band were very uncomfortable at the thought of cranks coming up to them, and when they went to America later they were plagued by dreadful cranks.'

They were also plagued by the spectre of their lead guitarist quitting the group. This disaster actually happened at the time when Jethro Tull lost their lead guitarist Mick Abrahams, who went to form Blodwyn Pig. Flute playing leader Ian Anderson was casting about for a replacement and had his eyes set upon Tony Iommi. With his own band still going through dark months of uncertainty, Tony could not resist the lure of joining a challenging, successful group like Tull. It was also very flattering, as Tull were beginning to break free of the blues and experiment and would have made great demands on Iommi's guitar playing ability.

Tony explained his decision later: 'I didn't really want to go and leave the boys but it seemed like we had come to a bit of a dead end and I rated Ian Anderson really highly.' As the shock of Tony's sudden departure began to sink in, the rest of the band wondered whether to find a replacement or just give up the struggle. But the agony was soon over. Tony came back and Black Sabbath survived.

'I only stayed with Jethro Tull for two weeks,' said Tony. 'It was just like doing a nine to five job. The group would meet, play a gig and then split. In

our group we were all good friends. We not only worked together as a group but we lived together. I just felt more at home with Sabbath. We were all friends and we all had similar ideas about how our music should develop. In Jethro Tull I wasn't sure that I would fit in all that well.'

It was rare indeed for an up and coming young musician to throw away the chance of instant stardom but loyalty prevailed. And there's no doubt he found Ian Anderson a hard task master – Martin Barre became Mick Abrahams' permanent replacement.

The short lived split occurred while the band were still Earth, but now with the return to the fold of their leader, the name change, and Jim Simpson's efforts to get the band to the attention of the London music business, it seemed their luck was about to change for the better.

Jim had received fourteen rejections by major record companies but at last hope loomed. The older established companies were beginning to wake up to their rather conservative image in an age of experiment and free thinking. Smaller independent labels like Island, Immediate and Charisma had been setting the pace for some time and now the majors

decided to set up their own apparently 'independent' labels to launch new groups and artists. EMI had launched Harvest which was the company's home from home for hippies, and had a suitably 'underground' flavour. Phonogram then got into the fray with their own new label called Vertigo which signed such groups as Manfred Mann's Chapter Three and Juicy Lucy.

In January 1970 Vertigo announced they had signed Black Sabbath. It was the start of a new decade and a new era in rock. During the closing weeks of December 1969 the band had been busy playing in Zurich and Germany and on Boxing Day they played in Carlisle followed in the New Year by spots on local BBC radio stations. Sometimes the money was as low as £25 an engagement and even after signing to Vertigo, it only rose to an average of £50 a gig but with an added fifty per cent of the takings at the door. This was to be a cause of problems and acrimony between group and manager.

But these dark clouds had yet to loom on the horizon. There was still a feeling of euphoria that at last the Sabbs were getting somewhere. The ball had been set rolling when the London based Tony Hall Enterprizes signed the group and the money was raised to make the group's first album. The tapes were then leased to Vertigo.

Explains Jim Simpson: 'After we got the 14 turn downs we got the album made at a studio off Tottenham Court Road on a four track machine. It was all they needed at the time! At the same time Phonogram were setting up Vertigo as a rival to EMI's Harvest label. They had originally passed on the tape, and were not very excited about it, but in the end they said they would give us a 12 per cent royalty deal. They took it as a roster filler. They already had records by Rod Stewart, Manfred Mann and Colosseum. We were in the second batch of albums they put out.'

If the record company bosses weren't all that excited about Sabbath, as Jim suggests, at least their promotion people did their best to stir up excitement. An early press release stated: 'Since changing their name to Black Sabbath the band have awakened in themselves an interest in Black Magic, and the most deeply affected is Geezer. One night he succeeded in raising a demon in a church yard and has been so terrified at releasing the hidden forces of the occult that he has sworn never to dabble in the black arts again.' These stories keep gossip columnists supplied with material for months. It was rumoured that Geezer, far from giving up his dabblings, had actually succeeded in invoking a demon on stage during a performance. If it happened at all, it was probably an irate roadie searching for a broken jack lead. It was also whispered that the band had a black ram for a mascot, with a diamond embedded in its forehead.

It was all wonderful stuff, black propaganda if not black magic. And to keep up the image, Vertigo released the band's debut album *Black Sabbath* on Friday, February 13, 1970.

They were described in their next press release as 'A new four piece outfit which has emerged from Birmingham, a group whose sound is original, a group whose highly individual conception of progressive sounds will very shortly bring them nationwide acclaim.'

'Musically they are completely uncompromising, and would rather starve than sell out to more commercial forms of music.'

The same month the band made their debut at Birmingham's progressive Mothers Club on February 6 where they went down a storm and were booked back for four more engagements. They had already broken the house record at Henry's Blueshouse, a record which had ironically been set by Jethro Tull. At least Tony could take comfort in the knowledge he had made the right decision to stay with the Sabbs.

The band presented an alternative to the progressive rock scene that was all the more effective because of its apparently natural roots. And there was no doubt that their lead singer was a star, and at the same time a man o'the people. It took some time before Ozzy himself could define his appeal and hold over audiences as it developed at those early gigs.

Ozzy was, and remains, one of nature's exuberant and unpremeditated souls who was constantly getting into scrapes. Jim Simpson remembers one incident when Ozzy tried to play the knight errant. 'He was always getting into trouble and most of the time it wasn't his fault. He was walking in High Street, Aston when he saw a couple of guys had got another one up against the wall. So Ozzy sailed in with feet and fists flying. He could put himself about alright. But it turned out the two guys were plainclothes policemen making an arrest. So I had to get £100 together to get Ozzy out of that one. But he was quite right really. He saw two against one and decided it wasn't fair.

'But Ozzy often came round to see me feeling very distraught, because he never had any belief in his own ability.' Jim totally rejects any suggestions that Ozzy has some kind of macho image, to apply the language of the Eighties to a late Sixties situation.

Instead he feels he has a 'manic compulsiveness' and that expressed itself in his early attempts to wear a kind of Wild West garb with cowboy fringes on stages. 'It didn't really work,' says Jim with a smile. 'He just lacked the right kind of grace, elegance, composure or style. He wasn't very much the Clint Eastwood type and he knew that he wasn't succeeding with that type of image. But what he DID succeed in was an area he wasn't even aware of, which was this compulsiveness. He had no inhibitions about his voice – he would just let it go. So Sabbath was like an early punk band in a way.

'Ozzy had no technical qualifications really. At least Tony and Geezer could play their scales or a B flat chord. Ozzy wouldn't know what a chord was if it fell out of the sky and hit him on the head. He knew nothing about music whatsoever. All he had was feel. But he had far more going for him than the rest of the band. The band, in my opinion, was purely Ozzy.'

This has been a bone of contention among Sabbath fans for many a year. Many felt that Tony Iommi also shared the major role in shaping the Sabbath sound and impact. But Jim is less charitable towards his old protégé than he is towards Ozzy. 'Tony tried to stagger everybody with his technical ability. In fact he is a very limited guitar player. Considering what he has to do to get what he puts out, he is limited. All his solos were worked out in advance and he didn't improvise. The solos sounded great, and were very effective, but musically speaking, he's not that good a guitar player.'

Good technically or not, the Sabbath sound with its increasing reliance on doomy chords and floor shaking volume meant that news spread swiftly about the new group but only word of mouth. In the early days there was very little national press about the group. Some have suggested that the group were 'absolutely hated by the press' but this was an exaggeration.

Most of the music press at the time was geared necessarily by editorial dictate to the bands and artists who were most visible in the charts. There was no conspiracy to keep Black Sabbath out of the limelight, although it must have looked that way to the folks in Birmingham desperately trying to get publicity for their unknown band.

The word of mouth transmission of news about Sabbath probably did them a favour as forever afterwards they were known as the band who had made it without any suggestions of hype or publicity overkill. And most of the reviews that greeted their first album were quite favourable. When it began to hit the national pop charts, then there was quite a spate of publicity and nothing to suggest there was a hate campaign.

But legends die hard. Black Sabbath were locked out by the media so the story goes, and that's the way it will remain in the public memory of their early days.

Certainly in their home town there was a stir among writers and musicians. One of the first to be intrigued by the band's impact was a popular local hero, Peter York, who had drummed with the Spencer Davis Group and also contributed the odd amusing article to Jim Simpson's irregular newspaper, Big Bear. Not surprisingly Sabbath were featured on the front page of the first issue.

Said Pete: 'The first thing that struck me when I heard Sabbath was Tony Iommi's guitar. Picking myself up from the hippy strewn floor of the Marquee I winced as Tony's original phrases hit me. . . . I know this embarrasses him, because he's that sort of person, but he has a style that is refreshing and non-derivative. You can't be detached from your instrument and still lay down music of worth. Tony's involvement is complete and effective.'

Pete had obviously been to London to join in the celebrations when his colleagues had signed to Vertigo and was overcome by the excitement of it all. He went on: 'Black Sabbath's main impact is as a group. They obviously all dig each other. Essential. Ozzy Osbourne doesn't cringe us all by doing the star routine, he just sings and reacts to his friends, and that's how it should be. Much of the impetus comes from Bill Ward, who plays so good with broken drumsticks that I am in two minds about buying him a new pair.'

York had played in a drum trio with Bill, and Bob Lamb of Locomotive, and admired his constantly improving drum skills, in sharp contrast to those who thought him 'a very basic drummer.' Said Pete the expert: 'Bill's improvement over the months I have known him is an object lesson those who wonder why their playing just doesn't happen. Bill has got stuck into his instrument and worked hard, and it shows. Next time I see him, I'll break his wrists.'

Pete also raved about the musical skills of the rest of the band and even compared Geezer Butler to Frank Zappa. 'He also plays better than most bass players, supplying a solid cushion for the explorations of the others. Improvisation is nothing without a foundation, and if anyone's going to provide that, Geezer, we want it to be you. Frivolity aside, this is an exciting group which has shocked me to attention a few times. They'll do the same for you.'

The rest of the issue was devoted to news snippets about various local bands, with Sabbath given strong prominence. A 'date not to be missed' was their debut appearance on John Peel's 'Top Gear' show on November 29, and there was much gossip about the quaintly titled Ffolly Jam Session at Birmingham University which featured Locomotive, Tea & Symphony, Sacrifice and Sabbath. Readers were asked to believe that Geezer Butler was refusing to venture out 'unaccompanied after dark' because of their researches into black magic, and Ozzy, for no particular reason anyone could devine, had tattooed a face on each of his kneecaps.

More important was the news of the release of the group's first single *Evil Woman* coupled with *Wicked World* on January 2, and *Black Sabbath* the album on January 23. There were some unfavourable reviews. Said one critic: 'This is Black Magic Music for the sick masses... To me this stuff has all been done a million times before.' But then the reviewer gets confused and says: 'The music is fine, in fact there are some very interesting breaks.' Another music paper review followed the same track and said: 'There's a diabolically pretentious poem inside the cover and the music made by this trio is the sort of thing you've heard a million times before. Lead guitarist Tony Iommi is so influenced by Eric Clapton, one wonders if said gentleman was hired for the session. Sadly unoriginal.'

But the music was not as 'sadly unoriginal' as the reviewing style of the critics, for it instantly struck a response from the nation's fans who by March had bought sufficient quantities of the album for it to reach the top of the charts.

Among those who shared in the excitement the band was creating was their producer Roger Bain. He had first heard of the Sabbs when they came to London to rehearse. Said Roger: 'I received a desperate phone call from a rather terrified caretaker at the East Purley String Quartet Appreciation Society, telling us his rehearsal rooms were not suitable for any of those "guitar things." It subsequently transpired that the poor man had a number of cubicles measuring six feet square and had arrived at work that morning to find four very hairy and ferocious looking gentlemen, together with a mass of amps and speakers, wedged into a cubicle next door to a man practising Ravel's *Bolero* on the viola! So my initial involvement with Sabbath was a frantic search to find a rehearsal room ready for the group to move into, at 10 am on a Monday morning.'

Bain first saw the band playing a gig at Henry's Blueshouse. When they had completed their first set of the evening, Jim Simpson introduced producer and group at the bar. Recalled Roger later: 'I immediately felt the same as the caretaker in East Purley! There stood four aggressive looking characters, like Vikings who had strayed from their long ship, who towered above their surroundings, with dark flowing hair and brooding appearance.'

When the band began to play Roger summed up their efforts in the forthright language of the musical profession: 'They have the biggest balls in Britain!' A strange and painful affliction one might imagine but doubtless he was referring to the tonal qualities of the band's performance.

Roger was astonished at their power and was not in the least disposed to disagree with Jim when the proud manager said: 'I'd like to get Sabbath to play alongside Zeppelin, and blast them off stage.' Indeed *Led Zeppelin II* had just been released to universal acclaim and was the album which guaranteed the other Birmingham band legendary status for the rest of the decade. But Roger was convinced Sabbath had the same kind of staying power. 'I rushed out to get a copy of *Led Zeppelin II* and fantastic though the Zeppelin album was, the "buzz" we got from listening to the various bits of tape that went to make up *Black Sabbath* resulted in the Zepp's masterpiece being laid to one side. But then of course, we were biased!'

Just as the fans who crowded into Henry's Blues House were bowled over by Sabbath, so was producer Bain, who spotted something that might have been a severe handicap to the group. 'Tony Iommi, who had been favourable compared by a reviewer to the great god Clapton, was missing the tops of two fingers on his left hand.' This was due to an accident Tony suffered while working with machinery, and he had to wear protective finger stalls to enable him to cope with the guitar strings.

'This made his technique all the more incredible to listen to, as if it weren't incredible enough!'

Roger also waxed eloquent about the rest of the band: 'Geezer really was my personal, all time favourite bass guitarist. The power which he managed to get out of that strange looking Fender makes one suspect that by his delving into the mystical arts he had somehow concealed the Royal Albert Hall pipe organ in his amplifier!

'Ozzy, apart from having two of the most unusual tattoos I have ever seen (those kneecaps again), and having a voice capable of riding over the wall of sound generated by the band, possesses the ability to do two things particularly well.'

'One is to improvise and sing logical words off the top of his head to a tune which he has never heard before and the second is the skill which he opens pint bottles of Newcastle Brown ale with his teeth'. Bill Ward impressed Bain as well and he claimed him as his 'all-time favourite drummer.' Bill was 'the motive power of the band whether he was taking a 25 minute solo or playing a quiet accompaniment to a solo guitar.'

The first time band and producer rehearsed together was in a school hall where they were unable to anchor the drum kit in the normal fashion, by hammering nails into the floor, because of the parquet flooring. 'Every time Bill hit the bass drum the kit moved forward a couple of inches and while the rest of us remained more or less stationary we would only catch the odd glimpse of Bill as he chugged merrily past us up and down the hall!'

Roger summed up his early impressions of the band: 'Heavy beyond belief, ominous, talented, humorous and yet totally unassuming.'

The album Roger produced actually entered the national charts at number 23 in March, 1970 and their black magic image ensured a spate of suitably would-be macabre stories. One musician who had taken a long term interest in the study of the occult was organist and bandleader Graham Bond, who in 1969 had returned from a trip to America to launch a new band. Graham had been writing songs about 'Holy Magick' for sometime and was intrigued by the new group and perhaps not above gaining a little publicity for himself, hard to come by as his fortunes waned.

Graham, despite his desperate need for gigs, keep refusing to work with them because he claimed he did not approve of their stance on black magic.

Graham said he was 'a white magician' who followed the right hand path. He was into the occult and mythology, and chastised Sabbath for dabbling with the unknown. In the event it was poor Graham who eventually faded from the scene, and died mysteriously, falling under the wheels of a London tube train in May 1974. Magic, black or white, was never much use to him, and Black Sabbath were patently quite prosaic about their involvement in the black arts.

Ozzy told a reporter from the Birmingham Post in March 1970. 'I just liked the name Black Sabbath because of the succession of vowel sounds.' And as for the cover of the album which showed a witch-like girl with long dark hair and a raven in a tree, Geezer was even more specific. 'We approved the cover, but it wasn't our design. We just thought it went with the name.'

When it suited them, Sabbath would join in the fun and games of providing suitable copy for pop press like the now defunct IPC weekly, **Disc** which ran an investigation into 'Black Magic In Pop.' It revealed that by the summer the band wanted 'to get away from black magic as fast as possible.' Said Disc: 'With their first album in the chart, and bookings flooding in, the band feel the time has come to shed the gimmick before it becomes harmful.' 'We usually have black candles burning onstage,' Geezer Butler told Disc. 'And Ozzy is having a red robe made. But I think we'll get away from the magic even though we're into it. We're frightened. And because of all the publicity about magic at the moment, we're scared that when we go to America people will associate us with it.'

Geezer explained how Sabbath went about writing their controversial material: 'We all get together to write. Tony gets an idea, and usually thinks of a name for a number and we all add pieces of music and it comes out as a song.'

Geezer continued his fascinating insight into the Sabbath construction method. 'Most of the numbers are based on a certain riff. We don't use a melody, just a raw type of riff. Tony usually writes the basic thing and the rest of us will put in the minor riffs. We're not a progressive rock band, we're a heavy pop group and we don't mind the word pop. It's all pop music, let's face it. All groups are pop groups. It's just that some pop groups are deeper than others. I think we're medium deep.'

Geezer disputed that the band were influenced by anybody else and admitted they were highly ambitious. 'We'd like to get established all round the world and then improve our music as we go along.'

Tony Iommi joined in the clamour to be disassociated with groups like Black Widow: 'People are bringing us down saying we are a Black Magic group. I think they must be getting mixed up with Black Widow. We don't do any sacrifices on stage, and we're not on a black magic kick. We wanted to do heavy numbers and the guitar riffs we worked out were more suited to evil songs than things about love. We play songs about black magic, but they are more likely to be against it than for it.'

Black Widow hit back by accusing Sabbath of 'cashing in' on their publicity. Jim Simpson hastily denied this and wrote to Disc in June to say: 'After all, Black Widow hired a power-publicist, a superstar witch, assorted virgins and in doing so created joint-image for the bands which we don't want.'

John Peel, the Radio One deejay who had featured the band on his Top Gear show thought that Sabbath were 'hedging their bets' on the whole topic. 'They still wear black shirts with huge crosses, write songs about black masses and so on.' John noted that several girl fans at a Sabbath BBC recording session had inverted crosses drawn on their foreheads and claimed they were devil worshippers.

There was no escaping it – Black Magic was the inverted cross that Black Sabbath had to bear. But they could at least enjoy the spectacle of the album selling 5,000 copies on the first day of release and staying in the charts for over 13 weeks. 'Things have been quite rough at times but it's finally all paid off,' said Geezer in May. 'It's all a dream come true for us.'

The music press were astonished that the band could achieve so much without any sort of underground support in London. In the Midlands and in Cumbria in the dim and distant past Bill Ward and Tony Iommi had once lead a group that even pre-dated Earth. The full force of their following in these Sabbath strongholds had been unleashed when the album was released.

But apart from their reputation steadily built up on club gigs, the group acknowledged the help they received from Vertigo's promotion campaign. Said Geezer: 'People were always asking us when our album was coming out, and I think Vertigo's advertising helped.' He had another explanation for the group's success: 'I think Tony's guitar playing makes us stand out.' Once again he expressed continued annoyance at the image the band had been saddled with. 'We're fed up with all this black magic fuss,' said Geezer. 'We had no intention of being like that when we called ourselves Black Sabbath. We just liked the sound of the name', he added, echoing Ozzy's sentiments. 'People like us because they want to listen to our music, not because of any black magic gimmicks. We only do two numbers about black magic in fact, and they are both warnings against it.

'The others are supernatural things about cosmic dreams and astral planes which have nothing to do with black magic. Everyone writes songs about love, and we thought it would make a change to write about the supernatural.'

Bill Ward joined in the renewed clamour of protest: 'Our music did seem to be more evil than a lot of other groups. But this Black Magic thing has really got out of hand. We are mildly interested in it, and people gave us crosses to wear, but that is as far as it goes.' And that was as far as it went, for the next ten years.

Black magic in pop

BLACK MAGIC has never been a topic to joke about, but in recent years it has been fashionably daring to dabble on the fringe of it. Various bands have incorporated aspects Black magic in their acts—one of them being Black Sabbath, who now want to get away from all that as fast as possible.

With their first album in the chart, and bookings flooding in, Black Sabbath feel the time has come to shed the gimmick before it becomes harmful.

"We usually have black candles burning onstage," says bass guitarist, Geezer Butler, "and Ossie—the lead singer—is having a red robe made."

The cover of their album is extremely eerie, and has an inverted cross inside.

"But I think we'll get away from the magic—even though we're not really into it," says Geezer. "We're frightened. And because of all the publicity about Black Magic at the moment, we're scared that when we go to America people will associate us with that."

Black Sabbath, Birmingham-based, with an average age of 21, started as Earth 18 months ago.

"After a year we found there was a pop group called Earth from Plymouth," says Geezer, "so we changed the name."

Personnel is: Geezer (bass), Tony Iommi (lead), Bill Ward (drums) and Ossie Osborne on vocals and harmonica. They write their own songs, which vary from exciting fast numbers to doomy things.

"We all get together to write," says Geezer. "Tony gets an idea, and usually thinks of a name for a number, and we all add pieces of music and it comes out as a song.

"Most of the numbers are based on a certain riff—we don't use a melody, just a raw type of riff. Tony usually writes the basic thing and the rest of us will put in the minor riffs."

They dislike the term "progressive music."

"People say 'progressive' and go into classical forms which have been around for years. It's a non-meaning word. We're a heavy pop group and we don't mind the word pop. It's all pop music, let's face it. All groups are pop groups. It's just that some pop groups are deeper than others. I think we're medium."

They say they're not influenced by anybody to their knowledge. They're ambitious.

"We'd like to get established all round the world and then improve on our music as we go along."

Last year they spent six months touring Europe, and are now negotiating to tour America. In eight months as Black Sabbath they have already acquired an amazing following in this country, and apart from particularly strong support in native Birmingham, they have an incredible core of fans in Cumberland.

Is the pop Black Magic craze a harmless gimmick — or does it spell real danger to groups and fans?

MELODY MAKER, March 14, 1970—Page 35

marquee
90 Wardour St., W.1 01-437 2375

Thursday, March 12th (7.30-11.00)
* WRITING ON THE WALL
* MORNING

Friday, March 13th (7.30-11.00)
* TONY McPHEE and the
* GROUNDHOGS
* SILAS

Saturday, March 14th (8.00-11.30)
* NUCLEUS
* ARMADA

Sunday, March 15th
CLUB CLOSED

Monday, March 16th (7.30-11.00)
Roger Swatkins of First Class Agency presents:
* BLACK SABBATH
* GRISBY DYKE
* STRAIGHT LACE

Tuesday, March 17th (7.30-11.00)
* JON HISEMAN COLOSSEUM
* BARBARA THOMPSON
* ART THIEMAN QUINTET

Wed., March 18th (7.30-11.00)
Peter Rice presents
* ANYTHING ACOUSTIC
* SUNFOREST
* ALUN HULL
* CONTINUUM

Eight-track recordings
marquee studios 10 Richmond Mews, W.1. 01-437 6731

GREAT achievement for Soft Machine — the first "pop" group to be included in the Promenade concerts. They're giving a 40-minute Proms concert on August 13 playing "Keyboard Studies" by Terry Riley.

An upset manager of Black Sabbath, Jim Simpson, phoned last week after reading Black Widow's accusations in Buzz. "I feel we're not cashing in but suffering from Black Widow's publicity," he says. "After all, they hired a power-publicist, a superstar witch, assorted virgins, and in doing so created an almost joint-image for the band which we don't want. It's only natural that we should redirect any black magic things back to the source, which is Black Widow. We don't want that sort of publicity."

Disc 13th June.

BLACK SABBATH are tired of being called a Black Magic group — and being likened to Black Widow.

Lead guitarist Tony Iommi phoned from Birmingham to clear up the confusion. "People are bringing us down saying we are a Black Magic group. I think they must be getting mixed up with Black Widow. We don't do any sacrifices on stage and we're not on a Black Magic kick.

"We wanted to do heavy numbers and the guitar riffs we worked out were more suited to evil songs than things about love. We play numbers about Black Magic but they are more likely to be against it than for it."

PEEL'S THOUGHTS

BY THE TIME you read this ("I refuse to read such filth"—Mrs J.N. of Water Orton) the Pop Proms will be half over. If you've missed any of them for any reason you'd better move at a cracking pace to catch the rest. This past week has been something of a treat as far as music goes. Last Thursday producer Jeff Griffin recorded Medicine Head and Black Sabbath for the Sunday (repeated on Wednesday) Show.

Medicine 'Head seemed a bit nervous but they sounded good. Black Sabbath disassociated themselves from the current Black Magic trendiness but still wear black shirts with huge crosses, write songs about black masses and so on. A certain amount of hedging your bets there.

Anyway there were several ladies in the front row at the Paris studios who told me that the inverted crosses drawn on their foreheads were an indication that they were "devil-worshippers." From weekend revolutionaries to weekend devil-worshippers. In the spirit of research which motivates every move I make I will endeavour to interview one of these devil-worshippers for next week's paper. Will she have "I love Beelzebub" tattoed across her? Find out next week in "Disc". Research can be fun.

Anyway Black Sabbath played well too. Safely — nothing very adventurous but the audience was well pleased with it all.

Top Ten L.P.s

1 (—) Live at Leeds (Track), The Who.
2 (2) Bridge Over Troubled Water (C.B.S.), Simon and Garfunkel.
3 (5) Deja Vu (Atlantic), Crosby, Stills, Nash and Young.
4 (1) Let It Be (Apple), Beatles.
5 (4) Andy Williams's Greatest Hits (C.B.S.), Andy Williams.
6 (—) Led Zeppelin II (Track), Led Zeppelin.
7 (—) Bumpers Double Album (Island), Various Artists.
8 (6) Black Sabbath (Vertigo), Black Sabbath.
9 (—) Tom (Decca), Tom Jones.
10 (3) McCartney (Apple), Paul McCartney.

CHAPTER 4
BLACK MISCHIEF

Success is a strange beast. It does peculiar things to people and they react in a variety of unpredictable ways. The phrase 'ego maniac' was readily absorbed into the rock world's lexicon during the boom years. There was much need of it as artists both British and American were caught up in the gold rush of hit records, sell-out concert tours, festivals and movies that hallmarked the Seventies.

To match the onrush of talent and its hungry world wide audience, there was a scramble to gain control of the most lucrative money spinners. The rock business was made up largely of wide-eyed success hungry youngsters, well-meaning semi-professional promoters, managers and record makers. Huge budgets were often in the hands of students promoting college gigs. Businessmen acting as managers for hot new groups found themselves caught up in a fast moving rat race where the rules were made up as it hurtled along. The guidelines were blurred and the whole business was ripe for a take over by the hard-nosed and ruthless.

But at the beginning of 1970 and during its early months there was no ego problem with Black Sabbath and the unexpectedly huge sales of the first album left everyone happy and excited.

Jim Simpson has fond memories of those early days. 'While I had them, success had not really penetrated. Just to get a couple of quid in their fists seemed great. And Ozzy was so grateful when we started to get some money. He'd say "Oh we're so grateful, if it hadn't been for you we would never have made it." He was almost over the top with gratitude.'

'Ozzy was a good, honest, straightforward guy, even if he got into a few scraps. He over reacted to situations, was slightly paranoid I suppose, but he was unspoiled by success. Tony was a bit more direct. He'd say "Right, we've got this far, what's next?" He came from a better off family than the others. They supported him and bought him nice new guitars when he wanted them, while Bill Ward had to scrape around to save enough to buy cymbals. He was always cracking and splitting them on stage.'

The rest of the band took the dawning of the Age of Sabbath in their stride. Says Jim: 'Geezer was very quiet about it, and Bill was quiet except he used to get horribly drunk. Ozzy was a bit of an outcast in the

group, even then, mainly because he wasn't a musician. Iommi looked down his nose at Ozzy a lot, and felt very superior to him. Iommi was very keen on being the star of the band and I think he resented Ozzy getting attention. I even think he chose Ozzy in the first place because he wasn't an accomplished singer. And in the early days Ozzy always felt grateful to be allowed into the band.'

Jim was aware of the subtle divisions and pressures within the group as he took charge of their affairs and embarked on his campaign to get them out of the blues clubs and into the national arena. There were endless business meetings and at them Simpson got the impression that Iommi and Butler had already made up their minds and decisions were taken well before the meetings. This somehow managed to override the five man voting system he tried to introduce and there was much behind the scenes lobbying on various issues with Tony and Geezer always trying to get their own way.

'Ozzy was the wild card that would just fall anywhere. But his opinions were never taken too seriously,' says Jim.

CARDIFF ARTS CENTRE PROJECT BENEFIT EVENT

THURSDAY, 5th FEBRUARY — 5.30-2 a.m.

SOPHIA GARDENS PAVILION, CARDIFF

PINK FLOYD

QUINTESSENCE
GARY FARR
HEAVEN
RON GEESIN

DADDY LONG LEGS
TEA AND SYMPHONY
BLACK SABBATH AND

Tickets 25/-

Free afternoon Concert for ticket-holders 2.30
TRADER HORNE — TONY CRERAR — POETRY
JAZZ — PUPPET THEATRE — EVENTS

Tickets from SOPHIA GARDENS BOX OFFICE, Tel. 27657 or STEVE ALLISON, STUDENTS UNION, DUMFRIES PLACE, CARDIFF.

Cymric Federation Press, Neville Street, Cardiff.

McILROY'S, SWINDON
MEL BUSH presents
Thursday, May 28th
BLACK SABBATH Admission 10/-
Thursday, June 4th
BLACK WIDOW Admission 6/-
Thursday, June 11th
CHICKEN SHACK Admission 10/-

at FOX ON THE HILL DENMARK HILL S.E.5
Wednesday, June 10th. 8.00
BLACK SABBATH
Bob Stevens D.J.
Licensed Bars — S.U. Cards
Next Wed GROUNDHOGS

MOTHERS
High St Erdington B'ham
Phone: 021-373 5514
YOUR HOME OF GOOD SOUNDS
FRIDAY, JANUARY 30th
FREE TO MEMBERS!!
PROGRESSIVE SOUNDS
ERSKINE & ROD GIL CHRIST
SATURDAY, JANUARY 31st — SCOOP! FROM THE STATES!
SPIRIT! - SPIRIT!
SUNDAY, FEBRUARY 1st
FAIRPORT CONVENTION +
IAN MATTHEWS SOUTHERN COMFORT
WEDNESDAY, FEBRUARY 4th
GORDON JACKSON AND FRIENDS WITH PADDY McGUIRE
FRIDAY, FEBRUARY 6th
JOHN PEEL with BLACK SABBETH
SAT FEB 7th **PENTANGLE**
TERRY COX BERT JANSCH JACQUI McSHEE JOHN RENBOURN DANNY THOMPSON
TICKETS NOW ON SALE

BLACK SABBATH and GALLIARD
In Concert this Sunday, May 17th, 7.30 p.m.
JEPHSON GARDENS PAVILION, LEAMINGTON SPA
Tel. 21251

The TEMPLE 33/37 Wardour St., London W.1.
FRI. MAR. 27 ALL-NIGHTER, 9 p.m.-6 a.m. 12/6
RARE BIRD
TRAPEZE — RAINMAKER
YOUR STABLE DIET — SIMON STABLE
PALE GREEN LIMOUSINE LIGHT SHOW
SAT. MAR. 28 ALL-NIGHTER, 9 p.m.-6 a.m.
BLACK SABBATH
GYPSY — SOUR MILK SEA
MYSTIC SOUNDS — JERRY FLOYD — PALE GREEN LIMOUSINE LIGHT SHOW
Enquiries: 734 9466

CARDIFF ARTS CENTRE PROJECT
Sophia Gardens Pavilion, Cardiff
Thursday, February 5th
BENEFIT CONCERT
PINK FLOYD
QUINTESSENCE DADDY LONGLEGS
GARY FARR HEAVEN RON GEESIN
TEA & SYMPHONY BLACK SABBATH
Tickets 25/- from Steve Allison, Students Union
Dumfries Place, Cardiff
Afternoon, 2.30-5.30. Free concert to ticket holders
TRADER HORNE TONY CRERAR

'But Ozzy was never one to hold his tongue. If he felt something, he'd say it.' Jim found Black Sabbath was not an easy band to handle at the best of times. He could get on splendidly with Locomotive and Bakerloo Blues Band but found Sabbath emotional and insecure.

The band dutifully carried on with the work that had been booked through Jim's efforts. In May they played in Germany again and also filmed for German television for which they were paid the princely sum of £25 together with a 16 mm print of their efforts. There was TV work in Belgium and Holland, but even while the album was roaring up the charts, they were still playing at the Greyhound, Croydon (on April 19), for £50 with fifty per cent of the door, for which they had to play two 45 minute sets. There were other gigs for the same money at such venues as the Farx Club, Potters Bar on May 23, the Pied Bull, Islington, London on April 20 and Crawley Arts Lab on May 24. On July 1 they were booked by Southport Round Table to play for £300, which seemed a bit more promising.

On August 26 1970 they played at the Fantasio Club, Dortmund for £330 and received the same fee the following day for another one hour show at Bielefeld. Back in Britain the money went up a little and they were booked to play Brangwyn Hall, Swansea on September 11 for £300 and at Newark showground on October 24 for £325.

One of the highlights of the summer was their appearance at the 10th annual Jazz & Blues Festival, held at Plumpton Race Course. They played on Saturday August 8 and received £300 — with no percentage. For those keenly interested in the minutiæ of rock, the rest of the bill included Family, Yes, Elton John and Humble Pie.

To the public at large it seemed that Black Sabbath must be coining it with all the stories of tours and chart triumphs that filled the pages of the music press. In July it was announced that Sabbath would headline an extensive tour of France, Germany, Switzerland, Austria, Holland and Belgium with Manfred Mann in a Vertigo Records showcase. And it was revealed that their second album *Paranoid* would be released on September 4. Their first album had by then been released in America and it was claimed it had already sold 40,000 copies.

Bill told reporters the band was working 'ten times harder' than before their first album was released. 'But we are really enjoying it. We didn't expect success but now we feel we have got something to live up to. We live music 24 hours a day, and we rehearse whenever we can. Wherever we play, we always try to give our best.'

The band went back to Regent Sound, the studios in London's Tottenham Court Road, where they had made their album debut, to start work on *Paranoid* in June. By then the first album had been in the chart for 18 weeks. Once again they chose to work with producer Roger Bain and this time they intended to drop black magic entirely from their group compositions. It was all part of the group's campaign to disabuse fans of the occult ideas their record company had so lovingly embroidered.

June was marked by an unpleasant incident in Newcastle. They had some equipment stolen during a gig, and later, while strolling through the town, they were attacked by skinheads. Tony Iommi was badly cut and bruised and his right arm was injured, which meant the group had to cancel a date in Croydon the following night.

But the club gigs had ceased to be of such major importance to the band. It was the year of rock festivals, which sprouted all over the country. Whatever the weather, (and that year it wasn't bad), fans packed bed rolls, joints and toilet rolls and set off for distant fields where they could laze on the grass and dig the music.

There were two festivals at Plumpton that year, including an earlier, non-NJF event in May which featured Sabbath alongside Julie Driscoll, King Crimson, Roy Harper and Ginger Baker's Airforce. There was the Hollywood Music Festival, actually held near Newcastle under Lyme, North Staffs on a site locally known as Hollywood, which starred — once again Family, Ginger Baker and also Grateful Dead, Mungo Jerry, Traffic, Colosseum and Sabbath.

In Munich in July they played at the Euro-Pop Festival with Free, Rory Gallagher, Atomic Rooster, Status Quo, Deep Purple, Edgar Broughton and even the dreaded Black Widow. In August they shared the bill with Jim Morrison and the Doors at a festival in Montreux, Switzerland, and there were more festivals in Amsterdam and Maastricht, Belgium. At all these events, even if their first single and album had been prematurely dismissed by some critics, Black Sabbath won considerable critical praise.

Sabbath were reaching a wider audience of rock fans who might not otherwise have gone out of their way to hear them. The result was that the bad boys from Birmingham blew several of the more prestigious groups off stage.

For example NME reviewed Sabbath at the NJF Festival thus: 'By the time Black Sabbath went on stage the festival was in full swing, and the atmosphere was building up. The Birmingham group began with *Paranoid* their new single which turned out to be a tasty piece of rock, but rather short. Idiot dancers were "own thinging" all over the place as singer Ozzy Osbourne freaked out more than somewhat and lead guitarist Tony Iommi delivered some startling passages. *Can It Be* and *Hand Of Doom* were followed by *Fairies Wear Boots* which the group's likeable manager Jim Simpson later said was a subtle go at skinheads.'

The same paper reviewed the Euro-Pop Festival and wrote Roy Carr: 'Black Sabbath surprised everyone with a most commendable set. One of the big names of the future.' Black Widow were also mentioned at the same gig and said Roy: 'Finally Black Widow brought the proceedings to a close with much expected rudeness.' In-depth rock reporting

Black Sabbath left to right: Geezer Butler, Tony Iommi, Bill Ward, Ozzy Osbourne.

was something of a fledgeling art in those more innocent days.

It was during this period that Sabbath began to build their incredible rapport with audiences and Ozzy developed his stage persona. A review of their Festival Hall concert in October told how the fans went berserk. 'Such was the fervour of the fans that the stewards gave up and let the kids dance in the aisles and rush the stage,' wrote Richard Green in NME. 'After Monday's spectacle there can be absolutely no doubt that Sabbath is among Britain's top groups. Forced by hordes of stamping, clapping, yelling fans who had no intention of leaving without an encore the group returned for *Fairies Wear Boots* and created unprecedented scenes. The audience was on its feet clapping hands in the air, a goodly crowd dancing at the front and some even made it to the stage. Peace signs were being given all over the place and even a real live Teddy Boy was bopping in the best 'fifties tradition. In the end, the houselights had to be turned on to stop the show.'

The band's typical performance of the period started with *Paranoid* and worked through to *War Pigs* which was Ozzy's cue to freak-out and Tony began his major guitar solo. It was the pattern they were to follow for the next six years or so, come hell and high court judgements.

The 1970 reviewer concluded his piece by observing: 'During *Black Sabbath*, a Quatermass-like rhythm takes over and at any time you expect to see horrible demons crawl over the top of the amps.'

The demons were closer than Sabbath or Jim Simpson realised.

As Sabbath's popularity soared, it became only a matter of time before there was a serious take over bid for the group's management. Jim Simpson began to sense and then to fear the worst. With the benefit of hindsight he realises he relaxed his grip on the band at the time when they became most vulnerable to a concerted assault by determined usurpers. Overnight he lost them, to a team of sharp operators from London. It was a body blow for Simpson and resulted in a long drawn out court case that dragged on for years.

'Looking back, I think Ozzy would look kindly on our relationship,' muses Jim. 'Tony Iommi would prefer to push it under the carpet and pretend it was never there. But it was my own fault that I lost the band, and the reason I lost them was very simple. A few people had tried to steal the band already. Either they had lost interest or I had managed to scare 'em off by waving contracts in their faces.'

But his new rivals were made of sterner, more ruthless stuff and employed considerable cunning. Jim was running his business by day and going to Sabbath gigs in the evening, and by now there were five or six a week. He missed out on regular sleep and found himself stumbling into work at 2 pm bleary-eyed, still partially deafened by the music and unable to think straight.

'I wasn't doing justice to the other bands I

managed. It could be said I should have dropped the other bands in favour of Sabbath, but you can't do that when you've got people's careers in your custody. You have to try to keep it all going.'

Deep down, there was also the feeling that Jim the jazz and blues fan, didn't really approve of Sabbath's increasing reliance on hard riffing and volume. 'I seemed to be spending all my time listening to music which I didn't find attractive. I thought the first album had a semi-cultural importance. Perhaps I'm being pompous, but it was a reflection of the times and the environment. I thought a lot of that first album, but not necessarily from a musical point of view. It reflected a city and its youth and energy. But then I found myself listening to the same set played night after night.'

'Tony Iommi's guitar solos right from the beginning were orchestrated,' reiterated Jim. 'He never improvised a solo. And I thought it was all getting a bit crazy.' This monotonous repetition which fans found so hypnotising actually repelled their manager. And his presence at gigs increasingly began to feel like a spell of guard duty rather than a pleasure.

'At that time my wife and I were getting on very well together, except that I was never with her, so going to Sabbath gigs every night was destroying my family life. I felt I was a policeman, hanging around backstage, making sure nobody would get to the band and try and take them away from me!'

Simpson finally told the boys he wouldn't play policeman anymore and suggested he would be more use to them in the office, on the telephone and getting work. He told them he was going to trust them and stop coming to gigs. They all said they understood. He lost them within three weeks.

'Suddenly they were accessible,' recalls Jim. 'I liked going to football matches and to speedway. I was a human being who wasn't going to cut himself off from social activity. In a way it was funny. The week we had the number one album, there I was, standing on the terrace, watching speedway and eating a home made steak sandwich. Things never got out of proportion and I was able to maintain a normal life style, which I was grateful for.'

But such normality had no appeal for ambitious young musicians. They were lured by the bright lights and promises of big houses and fast cars, which could be theirs if only they rid themselves of present incumberances.

Simpson's bombshell came in the form of a letter from a London lawyer instructing him that he mustn't make any further contact with the band — whatsoever. The letter arrived by first post on a Saturday morning, September 4, 1970, during a week when the first Sabbath album was still on the chart after 22 weeks, the second album *Paranoid* was number one and second single *Paranoid* was number two. Jim was dumbfounded. At only two o'clock that morning two of the group had been on his doorstep asking for a hundred pounds to get them to Liverpool that night.

Says Jim: 'They knew the letter was on the way. But they still came round for their hundred quid.' Jim reacted by taking the group and their new management to court, but in his heart he blamed himself for the disaster.

'In a way it was all my own fault. Nobody was at all interested in Sabbath at first. I really did build them from nothing and believed that the guys and I had some sort of rapport. Several people made incursions and the most serious was by Don Arden, funnily enough. His was quite a polite one and he sent Charlie Wayne as his negotiator and they had a few assignations in the local Wimpy bar. But Sabbath did turn that one down and stayed with me.' (Charlie was Carl Wayne, lead singer with The Move).

The ultimately successful pitch for Black Sabbath was made by Patrick Meehan and Wilf Pine, two enterprising music biz figures who had previously worked for Don Arden and left to bag Sabbath for their own management company.

They approached the band, gave them first class rail tickets down to London and met them with a rented chauffeur driven Daimler limousine at Euston. Next came champagne dinners at the Speakeasy, the legendary night club where the rough and ready lads from Birmingham could rub shoulders with the stars of rock. Meehan and Pine told the band they shouldn't be driving about in an old Austin Princess which Jim had provided and that they deserved much better.

Says Jim stoutly: 'The band had only JUST broken and within a couple of months they had graduated from the back of a truck to their own £1000 motor car. But they were impressed by these champagne dinners and were told I was screwing them, which I wasn't, and which was proved subsequently in court that I wasn't. But the group were told they should go to gigs in helicopters and not waste their time with cars. So Sabbath signed with them, and it was Meehan and Pine's first venture. They had no capital to speak of. I was told they had about £500 and they rented one of these offices you can have by the day in Mayfair to look impressive.'

Jim claims that under the deal the group signed with Meehan and Pine, they were paid £100 a week each, and were provided with furnished houses and had their grocery bills paid. 'Ozzy's house was in Edgbaston and must have cost around £15,000 in those days. They were also given motor cars. Iommi loved changing his cars. One was a Rolls and another was a Lamborghini. But here is the sting. To avoid tax, the cars, the houses and the furniture belonged to a company which was later taken to a Merchant bank and converted into cash. So the guys didn't own anything at all! When it came to the crunch and the group left Meehan, they lost everything.'

One of the sources of discontent with Jim's management that precipitated the group's departure was his insistence on fulfilling old contracts negotiated before their records were big hits. Thus when they were on top of the charts, they were still going out for apparently poorly paid gigs. 'I did insist on the guys doing every date they had contracted. If we had a date booked six months earlier, it was our fault for having accepted it for three hundred quid. More dates were pouring in so why pull out of those that had been advertised and agreed? I was really firm about that which in a way reflected on me afterwards. Because in court they said they were a £2,000 band doing £300 dates. In a year we had pushed the band from £35 a night up to £600 and then the records went smack into the charts, and we were offered higher paid gigs. But we *still* had to do the gigs we'd been taking weeks before. I explained that to the band in great detail, many times. They were picking up the cash on those gigs and dividing it four ways. And when they left me, they left owing substantial commissions. There they were earning £600 between them for one booking, and yet they would settle for a hundred pounds a week salary! I suppose really they didn't believe it would last.'

Jim guessed that Sabbath thought their run of luck would soon stop and they would eventually go back on the dole.

If they could at least come out of it all with a house and car each they would be satisfied. They grabbed what they thought was the main chance, just when Simpson was about to restructure his contract with the band. 'Contracts can be made to look horrendous, as if the parties can't go to the toilet without permission, but these things can be negotiated. A contract is only as strong as it's exploited and I never used to be heavy on contracts. I gave the recording to Tony Hall Enterprises and to give an idea of what it was worth, he sold it in the aftermath to Patrick Meehan for something like £660,000. He bought Tony Hall Enterprises which was, in effect, the Black Sabbath recording contract. Tony Hall was a lovely man but it would not be fair to say he discovered Sabbath or ever understood their success. He was totally bemused and bewildered.

'When Sabbath left me, I had totally water tight contracts, so I slapped a load of injunctions on them. But injunctions are hard to hold on people when they effect their living. These injunctions were to stop them working, unless they got their gigs through me. I couldn't sustain them and took recourse to legal action and it took years to come to court. It was all dreadful. At first I felt that if I could talk to the group logic would prevail but I was kept away from them. Wilf Pine stayed with them day and night.'

The battle between the opposing camps began to hot up and Jim describes it as 'A very nasty time. It was literally the 4 am 'phone call with nobody at the other end. That happened almost every night. I'd go to sleep again and then the 'phone would ring at 10 am and I'd panic, thinking it was the middle of the night.'

The campaign to warn Simpson off even drew into its net an old friend who Jim trusted and did not suspect was involved in any skullduggery. He was a man who bred old English sheep dogs and sold motor cars. They had been quite close but when the traumas with Sabbath occurred, Jim had not seen him for some years. 'We had drifted apart. Then one night he came down to Henry's. I was glad to see him and said "Let's go for a drink." Then we had a really weird conversation. We talked about nothing in particular at all. It was as if he had come to see me, but didn't want to talk to me. He knew I handled Black Sabbath but that subject was too painful to talk about anyway, it didn't interest me at all.' After twenty minutes of aimless, desultory chat, the old friend suddenly looked at Jim and said: 'They won't kill you.'

Simpson was astonished. And he had no idea who 'they' were. 'Are you talking about Black Sabbath?' he asked. Eventually Jim worked it out. He had bought a car from his old friend for Black Sabbath and they had collected it. They knew his name and address and had passed on the information to their

new management. 'In a roundabout way he was delivering their threats. And the punchline was that they wouldn't kill me, but they'd probably hurt me. It was all he wanted to say and it was like he'd learned the words. Whoever 'they' were they thought the threats would be more frightening coming from somebody I knew. They had obviously bought him. And it was frightening.'

More scares were in store. 'This sounds melodramatic. I live in a little house at the end of a court where everyone has got a car. Every morning I put my hand behind the accelerator on my convertible. I thought "Well, things can blow up." I was already nervous because of the 'phone calls and threats.' Jim took to leaving the roof off his car so that any blast would go upwards and at the worst he'd lose a limb rather than his life. How did he react to this kind of pressure?

'Stoic as I am, I reacted with abject fear. What could I do? I don't want to sound ineffectual, although I probably am ineffectual, but my upbringing and training hadn't equipped me to deal with things like that.'

'If I went to the police, what could I tell them? "I had a 'phone call at 3 am. It was the sixth this week and it's only Wednesday." I told my lawyer about it but all he said was "Oh they're just trying to scare you. There's nothing behind it." That's all very well, I thought, but you're not sitting there waiting for the calls. It was real Al Capone stuff.'

The case was eventually heard in the High Court of Justice, Chancery Division. First High Court orders were made against the group granted by Mr. Justice Whitford, following the receipt of the letter repudiating Simpson's contracts. He claimed he had each member of the group under seven year contracts and he was entitled to up to 35 per cent of their earnings. The judge ordered Pine and Meehan not to 'intermeddle' with or procure breaches of the group's contracts with Simpson. But the order could only remain in force for a week before another hearing.

The defendents – Sabbath and their new managers – put up a fight. The group said that between March and April 1970 they had told the Plaintiff (Simpson) they were 'extremely dissatisfied with his efforts to manage them, that they had completely lost confidence in him and that they were considering putting themselves under other management. They claimed that in July 1970 the Plaintiff had obtained £400 advance on record royalties to go to America to organise a tour for the group. Instead, they said, he went to Spain on holiday.

There were complaints about the sleeve of *Paranoid* and suggestions that their manager had displayed a careless attitude towards expenses. Jim had answers for all the accusations. Friends also rallied round and told how Simpson was an eminently honest man. Ironically there was also support from Wilf Pine who left Pat Meehan and went back to work for Don Arden. And it was Arden's lawyers who took up Simpson's case.

'Don helped me a lot,' said Simpson. 'He wasn't too happy with Pine and Meehan because they had left him to set up in business with Sabbath. Wilf signed an affidavit which gave evidence in support of us which was really the crunch. Meehan and Sabbath couldn't fight me any longer. When one of the defendents said what we were saying was right the case folded under their feet.'

Even so, Simpson still did not get the money he claimed. 'The law isn't so much an ass, as a pig,' he says bitterly.

'I learnt such a lot about lawyers and I've got no time for them. I had an offer from Patrick Meehan to settle six weeks before we went to court, for twenty-five grand. My lawyer said: "Don't even call him back." And yet I had been trying to contact Meehan, to serve him with summonses or whatever for years. And there he was suddenly coming to us. We had come to the crunch and the court case and he thought the best way out was to negotiate a settlement, which was not unreasonable. But I did as I was told and assumed that Lawyers with fancy offices in London knew what they were talking about.'

More calls came and the offer went up to forty thousand pounds to settle out of court, together with all Simpson's expenses. But he was repeatedly advised that he had a water tight case and would get at least one hundred thousand.

On the second day of the case Sabbath introduced extra witnesses including a musician Simpson had previously taken to court, also for breach of contract. This seemed to throw Jim's lawyers into confusion. He assured them there was no problem and the musician couldn't possibly have anything against him, and that he had won that case. But alarm bells began ringing.

'I realised then that my lawyers had begun to suss that the other side hadn't got the money. Now they were looking for some way out of it, without losing too much face. They told me "Thirty-four grand is all we'll get from them!" Yet Patrick had already offered me forty-five, plus costs, to be paid before the courtroom doors opened. Now all I was getting was thirty-five grand out of which I had to pay my own costs. And most of the settlement was against Meehan and not the band, which was so stupid. They were the ones who were earning. I got £8,000 on the day and £7,000 went straight to the lawyers for their fees. I got one thousand on the day and the rest is still mostly tied up with Don Arden's lawyers who took over the case when I ran out of money.'

Years later Jim Simpson bumped into Geezer Butler whilst out on a shopping expedition. They exchanged pleasantries. There was nothing more to be said.

CHAPTER 5
BATH TIME WITH SABBATH

'When are you going to get a real job?' That was the cry of father to son on learning the latter had joined a 'beat group' in the Sixties. Few could conceive that the horrible row their offspring were making was in anyway commensurate with earning a living. The traditional way, especially in the Midlands, was to get an apprenticeship in engineering and work through life towards a pension, with a powerful union on hand to guarantee the annual wage rise.

'Don't go into rock'n'roll business,' advised Dad, pressing Old St. Bruno into his pipe and swatting a fly with a rolled up copy of the Daily Sketch. 'It'll all end tomorrow.' Ah, the twists of fate. Since the recession, engineering has become a wasteland of redundancies and uncertainty, and music has survived and grown into one of the UK's few industries still offering security to its original workforce.

It took courage to stick with rock music when stolid values prevailed and the pressure was on to conform. 'So, one or two chumps have made it,' argued cynics, 'but it doesn't mean everyone can be a star.' Yet, it was those attributes not usually associated with feckless youth – toil and devout faith – which ensured Sabbath's ultimate triumph.

They might not have been prepared to knuckle down to a nine to five job at Amalgamated Screwings Ltd. and to suggest a pension as glittering prize to Ozzy Osbourne would be to invite scorn and possibly even a sharp blow to the nostrils. But the band were prepared to work and suffer the privations of long hours in dank night clubs, the modern equivalent of satanic mills, and to travel hundreds of miles, often to be ignored or reviled for their efforts.

They realised that as they played in the German night clubs they were on a training course with no guarantee of success at the end. When their first album was a hit, the band were still, as we have seen, playing places like the Star Club in Hamburg. Said Geezer, recalling the period with amusement: 'We used to read in the music papers that we were doing really well and we'd see our album going up the charts and all that. We used to think "We're really doing great" and then we'd look around at the places we were working in and begin to wonder if it really was our album. If it was doing so well in the charts why weren't we playing at all these big stadiums and all the big gigs throughout the world?'

Was this fiendish exploitation of talented youth condemned to long hours of drudgery at the hands of capitalist managers? Jim Simpson explains that the situation was not as black as it was painted. 'In those days a band would play in England two one hour sets a night. Is that testing? And you mustn't put it in the context of 1982 when you have an unknown band renting hundreds of pounds worth of PA and lights and playing to six people. In those days realism dominated. The bands played for a couple of hours and the kids paid a reasonable amount to get in and there would be over 150 in the club. And that's how Sabbath grew up – on a really full date sheet.'

But the rationale of management and the aspirations of artists are often poles apart and this was obviously the case with Sabbath for whom the logic of steady progress and 'reasonable' money had no appeal. They had done all that and wanted action. They were to see plenty over the next decade.

Such was the caution exercised around the band in their early days, that even when they changed their name to Black Sabbath in July 1969 they were still billed as Earth at some of their gigs in Cumbria. 'Their following then was all in the Midlands and the North. The South wouldn't touch 'em,' says Jim.

'We had to keep the name Earth for a while, because some places wouldn't use the name Black Sabbath. They were already really big as Earth. So the band went abroad a lot? Well they got regular money which they had never managed to get in England because it was very hard to sell an unknown band. At home they were still getting £25 a gig. In Germany they were booked for six weeks at a time, they got food and accommodation, and sometimes, they had to do six sets a night, but that was spread between 8 pm and 2 am. The Beatles used to do that too, so it was no harder on Black Sabbath. The only one it was hard on was Ozzy because he had no technique. So they used to play loads of instrumentals to save the guy's voice. Because technically he wasn't a good singer, he just blew it out after the first couple of sets.'

Simpson insists that when the band got back to England they were playing two 45 minute sets a

night, which was well within their capabilities. 'Iommi used to grumble like mad, because he's very lazy' says Jim. 'But Ozzy used to love it because he could pull all the women and get drunk. Bill used to like it for the beer and Geezer tended to accept the lifestyle without asking too much about it. Iommi used to bellyache about Germany but I told him he was fifteen times better as a musician and that alone was worth it, apart from coming back with some money in his pocket.'

The band had earned about £250 a week in the German clubs and with food and accommodation paid for, there were tangible benefits as well as succour for the soul.

'In fact we broke the band faster in Europe than we did in the UK' said Simpson. 'At home everybody thought we had bought our first album onto the charts. And yet without any press coverage, the first week we released the record, we had advanced orders of 5,500 from the kids all around the country.'

The grass roots following built steadily among Belgian, Dutch and German fans as they toured small clubs, but they still found inexplicable resistance in the South of England which was still hugely loyal to Cream and Hendrix and was suspicious of upstarts from the Midlands. There were even complaints made to the management that Sabbath weren't a proper blues band. In 1969–70 there could be no more damning indictment.

'We never used to get any bookings in the South, then after the record had been in the charts for a couple of weeks I managed to persuade Jack Barrie at the Marquee to book them, and there were queues down the street when we arrived. I had only got them on because the Marquee had done well with Bakerloo.' Sabbath played at the Marquee on Monday March 16, 1970 supported by Grisby Dyke and Straight Lace. But it wasn't the first time they had played there. On March 11, 1969 as Earth they had supported the Locomotive and Bakerloo at a Jam Session. Strangely enough the compere on that night was Tony Hall. Stranger still, a band called Black Sabbath were billed to appear two nights later at the Marquee on Thursday 13th supporting Terry Reid. How was it Earth could turn into Sabbath within 48 hours, and some four months ahead of schedule? Memories have grown dim over the years, and Jim Simpson cannot explain the anomaly. 'All I can say is that the Jam Session took place and the Earth billed was definitely Sabbath. It was part of the Big Bear Ffolly. It could have been that Sabbath had booked a solo gig under their new name, but I don't remember them ever playing with Terry Reid.'

Whatever the confusion about their early gigs, there was no mistaking the effect they had on audiences. And it wasn't just critics who were disturbed by their uncompromising stance. Legend has it that John Gee, the somewhat waspish manager of the Marquee told them: 'If you're going to play here again, you'll have to have a bath first.'

Earnest pop fans were shocked by volume rather than offended by grime.

Wrote one Jeff Churchill to a music paper: 'Having attended a performance by the newly acclaimed underground rock band Black Sabbath, I was disappointed that they, like many other bands in the same ilk, suffered from over amplification. A potentially exciting band was stifled by sheer noise and left serious doubts in my mind about their musical validity.' Tut, one might say, tut.

Caroline Boucher, a critic with Disc & Music Echo was equally unimpressed when she saw the band in action at the Marquee at their March 1970 gig.

'There isn't much Black Magic about Black Sabbath. The vocalist wears a red robe with a sign on the back and the drummer wears a crucifix, but that was the right way up. And although there isn't really a set of rules for what Black Magic music should be like, Sabbath's certainly doesn't seem to faintly resemble anything evil, mysterious, black or doomy. At London's Marquee on Monday, I was positively bored.

'As a group they have little visual impact; no accompanying mime like Black Widow. Singer Ozzy Osbourne, seemed obsessed with flopping his hair in front of his face so his facial features are scarcely visible for most of the time. Guitarist Tony Iommi played a loud and mainly meaningless guitar. Within minutes of going onstage he was doing sprawling, untidy guitar breaks, which continued through their hour's performance.'

Poor Caroline. She always did prefer horse riding to heavy rock. Nevertheless her reaction was sharp and the response pithy enough to give us a more accurate and detailed glimpse of early Sabbath at work than one might glean from a perfunctory spot of damning with faint praise of 'the band played a hard working set' variety. Continued La Boucher: 'And if the lyrics are something to write home about I'm afraid I missed those too, but this may have been due to the volume at which it seems imperative for speakers to be tuned to these days.'

'Their repertoire was samey, their musical ability insufficient to carry an act with only a bass, lead, drums and vocalist. Head banging volume doesn't make up for a bad basic sound. They seem to lack that rapport that links a good band to the audience. Black Sabbath seemed a very insular act, which may have been due to nerves but I was unmoved.'

Bill Ward once again endeavoured to explain to critics why they used volume in such an aggressive manner. 'It used to drive us mad thinking that we were playing and working hard while all these guys were sitting around chattering. So we turned up the sound louder and louder until it was impossible for anyone to hold a conversation.'

Jim Simpson holds slightly different views however. 'They got louder and louder for basically one reason, and part of the blame can be laid at my door. The band didn't have much presence on stage and volume seemed to be the way out. And Tony really wanted to get across the big guitar solo. Not long. Loud. Full. So we just kept on reinvesting in PA. The money we spent with Laney sound was phenomenal. And the reason was to get the power we thought was lacking. They hadn't got that much drive, so it was done by electricity. We started off with a 200 watt rig and built it from there.'

If the idea was to give a sense of power and importance to the music, it worked. 'Heavy' was the vogue word of the times and none came heavier than Sabbath. When Zeppelin started to break, the Sabbath management cry was that their boys made Led Zeppelin 'sound like a kindergarten houseband.'

'But we had an uncomfortable relationship with the media,' recalls Jim. 'While we desperately wanted press we didn't want the wrong kind, about black magic rites and all the rest. We wanted to be known as a heavy band.'

Despite the somewhat disparaging comments made about Tony Iommi by Simpson, and later by Ozzy, a great burden of responsibility rested on his shoulders for the projection of the Sabbath sound to the hungry masses. And he took his music very seriously. A left-handed guitarist, as Roger Bain had noticed, he had lost the tops of two of his fingers in a factory accident, but it didn't stop his ambitions to be a highly respected player. He had no interest in maintaining his previous jobs as office machines mechanic, salesman and welder. His pride and joy were his Les Paul Gibson guitars, which put through two 100 watt Laney amps and four Laney cabinets, gave him a greater sense of power over other mortals than magic could achieve.

Tony had started playing guitar at the age of 15 and his first electric model was a Watkins. He learnt to play by copying records by the Shadows and Buddy Holly, a practice followed by virtually all the major British players.

'Things were going great until one day at work I caught my fingers in a guillotine as I was cutting sheet metal,' he recalls. 'It took the tips off the two middle fingers of my right hand. I thought it would mean the end of my guitar playing. I had my hand in bandages for two months and I tried to play the other way round, but it was no good. I told the doctor that I wanted to play again and he said I would have to wait several months before I could touch a guitar again and he said I would have to wear some kind of covering over my fingers to prevent cutting them. He made me some plastic tips which were successful.'

Tony then put an advertisement in a guitar shop for a group to join and that was how he met Bill Ward, who was cheerfully dubbed 'Smelly' for reasons that have never been satisfactorily explained. It could be some form of American beat slang like 'He plays real SMELLY man.'

Tony used to play accordion as a child but later dismissed this phase as 'a joke.' His first love was the drums but gave them up when he realised he was never going to be really proficient, or even slightly smelly.

In fact the first guitar Tony Iommi ever used was a plastic Elvis Presley model. But he swiftly put away such childish things. 'I don't know why I got interested in music' he mused in an article he wrote in 1970. 'I just used to listen to the Shadows and wanted to play like that. I'll never be satisfied with the way I play. I'll always want to get better and better.'

One of the earliest criticisms Tony ran into was the oft repeated claim that he sounded too much like Eric Clapton. Was this but a case of pop reviewers mentioning the only other blues guitarist they had heard? Certainly Tony always refuted the connection. 'I don't think I'm copying anyone,' he said stoutly. 'I think I do my own sort of things. I just play what comes out. I can play what I am thinking but if I concentrate too hard I make mistakes. I used to practise a hell of a lot but I don't get the time now. I play what I feel and my influences are mainly jazz. We used to do a few jazzy things but nobody wanted to know. People wanted it heavy and we liked it like that. I think the group could go a lot further,' he said prophetically. 'But I don't know how it will develop.

'A lot of our things are just simple riffs and we get slated for that. But that's what we like and the way other people like it. I suppose I really thought I'd had it after my accident. I didn't think I'd be able to play again. But then I heard Django* and remembered he'd only got two fingers and thought if he could do it then there was no harm in me trying. Hearing him brought back my confidence.'

Thus emerged a familiar pattern noted in the development of all groups, that of early aspirations being tempered by practical considerations, and of compromise replacing heady idealism. Tony may have dreamed of being a fluent jazz guitarist, but found a quicker route to nirvana along the hard but golden highways of rock.

Delicate jazz lines on the guitar could not be expected to hold the attention of the mass of teenage fans hungry for the instant thrills and overwhelming power of amplified rock. This compromise and erosion of musical dreams did not mean that Sabbath's music, as it emerged during 1970, was in anyway a mindless, meaningless affair. The music expressed on the LPs *Black Sabbath* and *Paranoid* had great sense of form and clarity and was illuminated by a sense of purpose and direction. They had lowered their sights a shade, but they had focussed their view and the result was an intense beam of energy that seemed to bore into the souls of fans.

Over the passage of time those early albums now sound comparatively conventional in style and performance, but still the magic of Ozzy's voice and the fierce authority in the tone of the band's collective voice echoes down over the years and reminds how devastating it all seemed on first impact.

One of those critics who first looked intelligently at the heavy metal phenomenon pioneered by

---

*Django Rheinhardt, the Belgian gypsy jazz guitarist, recorded during the 1930–40s and was injured in a fire in his caravan.

THE CASTLE — WHITAKER AVE. RICHMOND
Tube: Richmond 5 mins.

SUNDAY, APRIL 19th
WE ARE PLEASED TO PRESENT
JUICY LUCY

SUNDAY, APRIL 26th
YES

SUNDAY, May 3rd
BLACK SABBATH

Lights by Frodo's Cinema - Sounds by Andy Simmonds - Many Bars

---

EEL PIE ISLAND TWICKENHAM
MARC NEWTON PROMOTIONS present

Fri. May 15 — **BLACK SABBATH** plus TINY CLANGER

Sat. May 16 — **SHY LIMBS** plus NEMESIS

Light Show Aural Plasma 995 3111 FREE PUNCH

KILBURN POLY. S.U. CHARITY WEEK DANCE
(in aid of National Children's Homes)

BLACK SABBATH
HARDIN and YORK
VAN DER GRAAF GENERATOR

Bar Discs Lights, etc.
Tickets: 12/6 adv., 15/- door, from above at
PRIORY PARK ROAD, N.W.6 (624 9369)
7 p.m.-12 Midnight
EMPIRE ROOMS, 161 Tottenham Court Road
THURSDAY, APRIL 16th
Tube: Warren Street.   Buses: 1, 73, 127, 253, N90

CIVIC THEATRE, DARLINGTON
Telephone 5774
Sunday, April 19th, at 8 p.m.
In concert
BLACK SABBATH
15/-, 10/6, 7/6

at the ROUNDHOUSE, Chalk Farm
SEVEN NIGHTS OF CELEBRATION
LIVING THEATRE ENVIRONMENT
GROUPS LIGHTS THEATRE
7 p.m.-midnight. Admission 10/-

MON., MAR. 9
QUINTESSENCE, GYPSY, BLACK SABBATH

TUES., MAR. 10
MARSHA HUNT, AUDIENCE, ALEXIS KORNER

WED., MAR. 11
DAVID BOWIE, GENESIS

THURS., MAR. 12
GRAHAM BOND, CLARK HUTCHINSON BAND
JUICY LUCY

FRI., MAR. 13
BRIAN AUGER, FORMERLY FAT HARRY, HAWKWIND

SAT., MAR. 14
THIRD EAR BAND, LIVERPOOL SCENE, KEVIN AYERS
& THE WHOLE WORLD

SUN., MAR. 15
ARTHUR BROWN, MIGHTY BABY, JACKIE LOMAX
+ HEAVY JELLY, PETER STRAKER & HAIR BAND
PRINCIPAL EDWARDS MAGIC THEATRE

Many more Groups unconfirmed at Press Date — stay tuned
SURPRISE GUESTS
Advance tickets at the Roundhouse from Wed., March 4

In the March 30th section of the HAMBURG EASTER FESTIVAL advertisement (presented by MECI-HAMBURG in association with FIRST CLASS AGENCY) which appeared in last week's issue of MELODY MAKER, the group BLACK SABBATH was inadvertently omitted.
The concert for this date should read as follows:
30th March, 3 p.m. till midnight
SPECIAL GUEST APPEARANCE OF
RENAISSANCE
BLACK SABBATH
GREATEST SHOW ON EARTH · WARM DUST · STEAMHAMMER
GROUNDHOGS · FLAMING YOUTH
KILLING FLOOR · SPHINX TUSH · PLUS OTHERS

---

marquee
90 Wardour St., W.1 | 01-437 2375

MELODY MAKER, September 12, 1970—Page 41

Thursday, 10th Sept. (7.30-11.0)
★ **GRANNY'S NEW INTENTIONS**
★ ARMADA

Friday, 11th Sept. (7.30-11.0)
A & M Records Sales
Convention, invitations only —
Free from Marquee Box Office

Sat., 12th Sept. (7.45 p.m. night)
Disco/Dance Night
★ **CUSTERS TRACK**
★ D.J. Bob Harris

Sunday, 13th Sept. (7.30-11.0)
SEE BELOW

Monday, 14th Sept. (7.30-11.0)
Vertigo Presents
★ **GENTLE GIANT**
+ GUESTS

Tuesday, 15th Sept. (7.30-11.0)
★ **BLACK SABBATH**
★ THE DOG THAT BIT PEOPLE

Wednesday, 16th Sept. (7.30-11.0)
★ **WISHBONE ASH**
★ ARCADIUM

MARQUEE STUDIOS CLOSED IN AUGUST FOR RE-BUILDING
RE-OPENING IN SEPTEMBER
DETAILS TELEPHONE 01-437 6731

MARQUEE SUNDAY SPECIALS by STRATTON-SMITH
Sunday, 13th: **THE WORLD**
ROGER RUSKIN SPEAR'S
GIANT KINETIC WARDROBE
Sunday, 20th: **LINDISFARNE**

Page 26—MELODY MAKER, July 11, 1970

KLOOKS AT THE LYCEUM

OPENING FRIDAY, 17th JULY
7.30 p.m. to 1 a.m.
A Festival Every Friday
FRI., 17th—London Debut of new
YES
BLACK SABBATH
CLARK HUTCHINSON
URIAH HEEP
BIG LIL

---

marquee
90 Wardour St., W.1 | 01-437 2375

Thursday, May 14th (7.30-11.0)
★ **BLACK SABBATH**
★ BAKERLOO

Friday, May 15th (7.30-11.0)
★ **SPIRIT OF JOHN MORGAN**
★ GRANNY'S INTENTIONS

Sat., May 16th (7.45-Midnight)
Disco/Dance Night
★ **HARMONY GRASS**
D.J. BOB HARRIS

Sunday, May 17th (7.30-11.0)
★ T.S.S. Presents
★ **AUDIENCE**
★ SUNFOREST

Monday, May 18th (7.30-11.0)
★ Peter Abbey Presents
★ **GRACIOUS**
★ LITTLE FREE ROCK
★ GINGER JOHNSON

Tuesday, May 19th (7.30-11.0)
★ **HARDIN YORK**
★ URIAH HEEP

Wednesday, May 20th (7.30-11.0)
★ Trident Promotions Present
★ **T.2.**
★ CASTLE FARM

DUNSTABLE CIVIC

SATURDAY, JULY 18th, 7 30-12
BLACK SABBATH

SATURDAY, JULY 25th, 7 30-12
WHO

Advance tickets for this concert are available by
sending a P.O., not cheque, for 20/- and S.A.E. to
Who Tickets, 15 Melbourne Road, Ilford, Essex

SATURDAY, AUGUST 1st, 7.30-12
FREE

GUESTS LIGHTS SOUNDS DRINK

Sabbath, was the American journalist, the late Lester Bangs. In a Rolling Stone article on the subject he rejected the prevailing opinion that 'all heavy metal groups sound alike.'

But he tended to go along with the belief that the sound the band and others like them made was not music. Wrote Lester: 'As its detractors have always claimed, heavy metal rock is nothing more than a bunch of noise; it is not music, it's distortion — and that is precisely why its adherents find it appealing. Of all contemporary rock it is the genre most closely identified with violence and aggression, rapine and carnage. Heavy metal orchestrates technological nihilism, which may be one reason it seemed to run dry in the mid-Seventies. It's a fast train to nowhere which may be one reason it seems to feel so good and make so much sense to its fans.'

In a guide to HM he called Sabbath 'sub-Zeppelin British kozmik behemoths.' It was this ready use of dismissive labels, usually administered with less skill and imagination, which coloured British rock writing throughout the late Seventies and helped alienate music press from its readership and often from the musicians. Mr. Bangs went on to predict the demise of the whole movement, just when it was on the verge of its greatest expansion. Yet only a few years earlier in 1972 he had written of Sabbath: 'Despite the *blitzkrieg* nature of their sound, Black Sabbath are moralists, like Bob Dylan, like William Burroughs, like most artists trying to deal with a serious present situation in an honest way . . . they are a band with a conscience who have looked around them and taken it upon themselves to reflect the chaos in ways they see as positive.' (Creem, June 1972).

When Sabbath eventually arrived in America they became wonderful vehicles for critical analysis. There were all the aspects of black magic and the 'teenage wasteland' to explore. We were told that Sabbath related to 'the entire depressing English working class experience. Sabbath is fighting against that background.'

It would have spoilt the effect of many a beautifully constructed essay if authors and readers had known that the name of the hotly debated group was chosen largely on the strength of the way the vowels and consonants flowed, and their image was the result of the fevered imaginings of an unsung but creative record company PR. But the day writers and fans stop reading significance into the actions and pretentions of the objects of their affection and scrutiny, will be the day rock'n'roll dies.

In summer '70 plans were advanced for the band to go to America. This was the big one. Expectations were high, and the boys were excited at the thought of following in the footsteps of Cream, the Experience and Zeppelin. Fortunes awaited in the cities of the plain where lurked huge concert halls and millions of teenagers ready to yell 'right on' and with money to burn on tickets and albums. There was also that sense of commitment and loyalty American fans bestowed with such generous enthusiasm on those English groups oft bruised and battered by blasé attitudes at home. England spawned groups. America nurtured them and ensured their survival.

At first they were due to go in August 1970 but the dates were postponed until October because of 'the fear of student riots' which sounded like an excuse for behind the scenes failure to secure appropriate contracts. Their first album was released in America on Warner-Reprise and sold more than 40,000 copies in two weeks. Obviously there were enough potential Sabbath fans to make a visit worthwhile. Reported Melody Maker in June. 'Their four week American tour due to start at the beginning of August has been cancelled because of the closure of Fillmore West throughout summer. The organisers anticipate student troubles if a large crowd gathers there . . . a spokesman said the group were all very disappointed at the cancellation.'

While efforts were made to reschedule their trip the band were kept busy with European festivals and tours and gigs at home like their appearance with Yes at London's Lyceum ballroom on Friday July 17. Roy Carr from NME was there and said: 'First success went to Sabbath who have improved beyond all recognition and are building up a strong, loyal following. Singer Ozzy Osbourne performs like a man possessed. Apart from featuring well received cuts from their first album they also presented a couple of songs from their next most noteworthy being *War Pigs* which included some intricate interplay between lead and bass guitarists Tony Iommi and Geezer Butler, during which drummer Bill Ward laid down a thundering beat.'

'Audience reaction gets better and better and we get more excited with the success that seems to be coming' Tony Iommi told the MM that same summer, as he discussed the release of *Paranoid*. Said Tony: 'We like heavy music and we feel that it's going to go on for ever and ever. You can drive a lot home with heavy stuff, get into what you mean to say, and we are totally satisfied with the way the sound is going. *Paranoid* took only a matter of hours to produce. It was all just an instant thing, spontaneous. There was little written down. People still expect us to sacrifice virgins and occult things like that, but if I say it once, I'll say it a thousand times, it was never anything to do with us.'

If Tony was still busy denying magical connections at home that summer, then he had to repeat a thousand times more when the great American public finally took the band to its bosom in the autumn. Their first visit was a three week tour which started in Philadelphia on October 30. TV appearances were also lined up to promote both tour and *Paranoid* single.

Their new managers, Patrick Meehan and Wilf Pine planned a British concert tour by the band for February 1971 and they also got them a spot on **Top Of The Pops** when they shared the bill with Diana Ross, Family, Engelbert Humperdinck and

Cliff Richard.

But even a close encounter with Cliff on **Top Of The Pops** could not eclipse the excitement the group felt about the States. There were concerts planned for the Detroit Olympic Stadium (November 7), and New York Fillmore East (10), as well as five days at the Whiskey A Go Go, in Los Angeles.

Tony Iommi told NME's Richard Green that he was looking forward to seeing bands like Blood, Sweat & Tears and Chicago in the States, but there were also a few lurking fears. 'We're worried about this black magic bit in America. People might take it seriously. We might change some of the words of the songs so that we don't have any trouble! If we get the time I'd like to see Joe Pass. He's a fine guitarist and one of my early influences. It's people like him and Alvin Lee that I like, who have got a style of their own. You can listen to them and think "I've never heard that before." They have their own thing going without having all these Clapton things creeping in?

Geezer was also anticipating problems on that first US trip and said: 'We just hope we don't get all this black magic confusion over there. We are frightened by the thought of the extremists. We don't want anything to do with the Charles Manson thing.' (The Sharon Tate murder case was hot news at the time). We will just be going over there as a British hard rock band. We are now in a position to tell the publicists and record company what to say. Before we were just another band. In the States the album cover will just have a picture of the band instead of an inverted cross.' Geezer claimed that already American witches had been 'phoning the band and trying to book them for black masses.

Geezer rammed home 'the truth about Sabbath' once again in an interview in Music Now magazine. 'We got the group's name from the title of a song we wrote called *Black Sabbath*. What with that magazine **Man, Myth And Magic**, it looked like people were starting to associate with Black Magic in a big way. The song was a warning against that. We were just telling people to stay right away from that scene. In all the confusion, people ended up thinking we were trying to turn them onto Black Magic when we were trying to do the opposite.'

But just before the band went off to America, aggro threatened the band, not from American witches, but from a local British rock promoter who was rather upset when the band failed to turn up for the Newark pop festival. This was a 12 hour show held in October 1970 called the **Festival Of Contemporary Music** which was a small time attempt to compete with the year's rash of events like Hollywood and Plumpton. It was attended by just over 1000 fans and the tempting fee of £325 was expected to lure the band down to perform. Indeed the organiser said he had a contract drawn up a month earlier which guaranteed their appearance. But the group were under new management who were not so fussy about low paying gigs booked under the previous regime. The band had just had injections for their first trip to America and were not about to dash down to Newark.

The top billing was handed over to a local group Cherokee Smith, who according to reports 'went down a hit in their place.' It was tough on the waiting fans but then Sabbath had been 'doing the right thing' for a long time and could not be blamed for conserving their energies for the golden opportunities that lay further afield than Newark. But if they had gone to that particular festival, they might well have experienced the kind of teenaged hysteria that was unexpectedly plaguing the group on their last British dates before heading for the States.

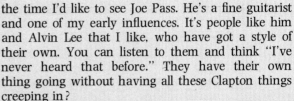

CHAPTER 6
LET SLIP THE PIGS OF WAR

A strange thing happened to Black Sabbath on their way to the theatre. They became overnight teenybop idols. It dawned on them just weeks after their appearance on **Top Of The Pops** with *Paranoid*. Little did the long haired, greasy rock musos know there was an audience of mini-fans who could not broach the security of the kind of premises they had been playing since their inception.

A 13-year-old girl could not visit the Star Club or Henry's Blues House, except perhaps in the most dubious circumstances, but they could watch telly and buy tickets for the first public concert that came to town. Young teenage fans were expected to be swooning at the sight of T. Rex or the Monkees. Yet a sizeable proportion of them were turning onto the forbidden fruit of the wild bunch from Aston. They too held aloft Sabbath crosses and gave peace signs. And when it came to piercing screams, they could out-shriek any of the witches of hell.

The band were confused at this sudden development, and their only good looking member, Master Ozzy reacted in some embarrassment when confronted with the facts. 'What a fucking drag that is,' said Ozzy just before their departure to the States. He had first noticed it at a gig in Portsmouth in September. 'We opened with *Paranoid* as usual and suddenly the place went potty. There were kids rushing down the front and girls screaming and grabbing us. We couldn't believe it – it was just like the teenybopper era all over again. We don't need fans like those. But we'll just have to grin and bear them and they'll go away. We're not changing our stage act to please the kids who just bought the single and it doesn't take long to find out who your real followers are.'

Churlish sentiments perhaps, but the band were clearly unsettled. After the long years of being gawped at by unmoving Germans and having the mickey taken by smart-ass critics, this kind of hero worship was almost too much to take. 'I think the reason we appeal to so many people so instantly is because our sound is good and basic,' thought Ozzy. 'It doesn't take a lot of understanding. The impact is right there. Of course we were choked off with the reviews and we began to wonder if we had done the right thing. But we had a tremendous hard core following in places like Carlisle and Workington

in the early days and they were the ones who bought our album when it came out. I guess the others follow out of curiosity when they saw it in the chart.'

With girls tearing at his clothes and screaming 'Ozzy!' the star paused to reflect. 'When we started the record companies didn't want to know. They wouldn't even take the trouble to listen to our tapes to see if we were any good. We were dismissed point blank. And we went through some really bad times.'

Tony Iommi helped Ozzy recall them: 'I can remember when we had to cancel rehearsals because we just didn't have the money for bus fares to the rooms. Or one occasion when Ozzy walked all the way to a rehearsal in bare feet because he didn't have any shoes. We had to buy him some out of our communal kitty, and that meant we couldn't buy any petrol for our old van. I know it sounds terribly phoney but it's all true!'

If the group seemed a bit short with their new fans and the breakthrough in acceptance it was probably because of the irony of this sudden new found popularity. It didn't seem long ago to them that a promoter in Carlisle was telling them it was impossible to find work for them because 'the kids couldn't dance to our music.' On that occasion the group gave in and played some dance tunes. But that resolution lasted less than one night. Said Tony: 'We played two pop numbers, couldn't stand it any longer and went back to our normal routine.'

Ah, sweet memories, and there was more nostalgia in the air as the band looked back across their then short career. They chortled about the way they hung around the Birmingham clubs hoping against hope that the top of the bill group would fail to turn up, so they could sit in and fill the gap.

'It didn't work very often,' admitted Geezer, 'but once we managed to get on stage when Jethro Tull were late arriving. When they did get there Ian Anderson said: "Well you had better let them carry on, because they're better than we'd be anyway!"'

Ozzy bemoaned the increased pressure success brought in its wake, as his valuable ligging time was taken up with photographic sessions and interviews. 'Now getting on stage and playing is the easiest job of the day,' he complained.

Tony Iommi also detected problems that accompanied success, 'People are already saying that we've sold out because the records are successful. It's ridiculous. No one is more surprised at the reaction than the band. We still don't know why both records were hits, we still can't believe it. There just doesn't seem to be any reason and we certainly never thought they would be when we recorded them. In fact we hadn't even written *Paranoid* until we got into the studios, and from then, it took us literally five minutes to put it and another track on the album together. We never plan any of the material and we've none for use on a future album. I might come up with a few riffs at some point that we could include at a later date, but it's not a conscious thing. On the other hand, the lyrics, when we write them are important. They say what the band really feels.'

So much for well constructed arguments about their essential working class ethos and reflections of a hostile environment... 'We leave it all to fate,' said Tony. 'The track on *Paranoid* called *Planet Caravan* is totally unlike most of the stuff the band does. If anything it has jazzy leanings. It was just nice to do something different.'

'If anything on the album is entirely typical of Black Sabbath, it's *Iron Man*. It's only because we haven't tried to go in one direction or another that we've got where we are. We can maintain a certain standard on stage because we don't try and complicate the music by bringing in instruments and phrases that aren't entirely natural to us.

'Our success has been the result of a lot of luck with *Paranoid* and we don't intend to try and recreate it. If you stop and analyse the numbers and attempt to reproduce something that they contained with an eye to the charts again, it's fatal, so you could honestly say that the hits are nice, but that's it, they will have no effect whatsoever on our future material.'

And of course, he was right. They were not to enjoy another hit single for many moons. The American trip turned out to be pretty much an introduction, and they discovered as many a group had done before them, that a hit or two in America still left vast chunks of the population totally ignorant of your existence. They played well and got a good response but they had to go back — soon, and in spring 1971 the band began the real grind of playing support to other bands and fighting for their own headlining spots. And then came the release of their third album *Master of Reality* by which time they could boast a fanatical following that was international.

The new album came out in the summer of 1971 and consolidated their image as purveyors of doom rock which to some American ears seemed almost sadistic in the delight it took in provoking feelings of gloom. Bill Ward sensed that this message touched the hearts of adolescent boys, notoriously prone to bouts of despair induced by recalcitrant girl friends and irritating parents. 'Most people are on a permanent down,' he said, 'but just aren't aware of it. We're trying to express it for the people.'

Despite all Jim Simpson's efforts he could not hold on to his old group, and in September 1970 they entered into a new management agreement with Pat Meehan and Wilf Pine which was to last for the next four years or so during which time Sabbath became one of the highest paid top draw bands in America. Whatever problems they subsequently endured with their new management, eventually their own hard work, constant touring and huge album sales brought riches and a sensational transformation in life style for the people's band.

As the decade began they still had to fight the

timidity and suspicion of the Establishment not to mention the misunderstandings that dogged their image and business activities. Their concert at the Royal Festival Hall on October 26, 1970 was a triumph. It had quelled their fears of London. When they first came to the capital they admitted: 'It scared us. When we first played at the Marquee we were all nervous. We thought London was so big we could die and nobody would notice,' said Ozzy. If it wasn't for the friendly help of Ric Lee of Ten Years After (the group's drummer), who put in a good word for them with the Marquee's management and ensured they got another booking, they might have retired hurt and baffled.

In the event London and the South fell to Sabbath's onslaught. The ultimate accolade was to be a performance at the Royal Albert Hall on January 5, 1971. But the great Victorian palace of culture had been redecorated and doubtless the management had heard on the upper class grape vine of the riotous reception accorded the band at the Festival Hall. They refused to accept the booking. It was a major snub. Thus their tour began at Hull on January 7 and went on to Birmingham (8), Bristol (9), Southampton (11), Sheffield (14), Edinburgh (15), Aberdeen (16), Newcastle (18), Nottingham (19), Manchester (20), and Leeds (23).

They were supported by Freedom led by Bobby Harrison, Procol Harum's ex-drummer, and tickets went on sale at eighteen shillings, or 90p in modern coinage. It was all part of the band's 'fair deal' policy, which today sounds like economic madness.

Although as we have seen Sabbath had powerful allies among the critics, who had encouraged the band with good reviews of concerts during 1970. Now success meant they came to the attention of hostile commentators who could not understand the appeal or the music. They reasoned that audiences, if they had any sense, and had been digesting their writing thoroughly, should have been listening to polite folk rock or progressive music. The concept of Sabbath, with its simplistic beat and apparently hysterical audience reaction was either laughable, or frightening.

When the band released *Master Of Reality* it came in for a drubbing, particularly at the hands of Melody Maker's Roy Hollingworth, who managed to be both whimsical and savage in his assessment of Sabbath's third.

'Packed in a doomy cardboard envelope, which one could well expect to contain an invite to a Boris Karloff housewarming, Sabbath turn in what might be called a loudly bleating length of self-indulgence. Apart from the acoustic introduction to *Sweet Leaf* (I thought they had sold out for a minute), this is just a conspiracy against any attempt to further the aims of hard bumping.' The rest of the review contained obscure references to laundry and steam engines and it is doubtful whether Sabbath appreciated or understood any of Roy's little jokes. Until now Sabbath had shown great forebearance with their critics. Ozzy might shout the odd 'Bollocks!' on glimpsing a review backstage but the group's public relation had been remarkably restrained. Now they showed their true feelings as Brummie good cheer was replaced by a certain petulance.

'A group gets on and people help them but when they reach a certain level, they start to slam you,' said Ozzy grinding his teeth in January 1971.

'Before they were slamming us they were slamming Led Zeppelin. Sometimes I get annoyed about it when the criticism has no point, when it is not constructive. On the whole we grin and bear it but I don't see why we should be knocked all the time.' Ozzy hated the way currently successful bands were consistently knocked in sneering tones. And he defended their own chart success. 'We strongly believe in our music. We don't do it because we like being pop stars. We were proud about having a hit single.'

Their uncharacteristic ill-temper was exacerbated by the increasing work load, as Meehan and Pine went to bat, and lifted Sabbath into the big league and away from the small clubs of 1970 for ever.

Work on *Master Of Reality* had begun with recording sessions at Island Studios in Notting Hill in January after they returned from the European tour which had taken them to Germany, Switzerland, Holland, Belgium, Denmark and Sweden. This bout of work came straight after their first American visit and said Ozzy: 'We need a rest badly. We're all very tired. We've never done travelling like we did in America.'

There was only a short rest at Christmas and then it was back to preparing three new numbers for the LP.

'People find it hard to believe but I reckon I do three times as much work in a band as I would in a normal job,' protested Ozzy. 'In America I had to go into hospital because my nerves were getting into such a state. It was all the travelling that shook me up.' For the first time Ozzy had discovered the meaning of jet lag, and endured the six thousand mile hop from New York to L.A. and back once too often for comfort.

'When we started, we didn't do too much work,' said Ozzy, 'but when the records started to sell it went from two gigs a week up to seven. That's when you get hang ups with people trying to hassle you all the time.'

It certainly was an unnatural existence, experienced by many of the newly successful. When a bus ride round the Bull Ring to the nearest pie shop was replaced by jet setting and high living in America, the result was mental and physical strain. But at least the group could share the experience and said Ozzy with great sincerity. 'We're all four together — like brothers. And that's because all four of us create our sound.'

Tony Iommi was swift to reject criticism of the band's new LP, and claimed it was the heaviest they had ever done. He thought that fans had been

disillusioned with Led Zeppelin's controversial third album, but theirs would offer no let up in the power. 'If we ever did decide to go acoustic with this band we would do it gradually. But at the moment, people want heavy music – the heavier the better,' said Tony wisely.

In April they returned to America and this time enjoyed rave reviews. *Paranoid* was a hit, and got to number eight in the Cashbox album chart and advance orders for *Master Of Reality* ensured gold status before it was released.

It was then the band earned its first dollars. 'The first American tour was really like an experiment,' said Tony Iommi, just before the band fled to a Welsh country cottage for some peace and quiet.

'We got there and played as well as we could, and let people see what we could do. It was hard work but it was successful. The second tour came as the LP was released, and it was really great. We played very well and that helped the LP get away. The first tour was to small venues and the second one was to 20,000 seat stadiums – and we filled them.' Tony had made the discovery that many other British musicians had made – that American fans' dedication was heartwarming.

'The kids in America are more into it. We have great crowds here, but American kids are prepared to go further. They are more concerned about the band as people – they like to know all about you.' The group were already being beseiged with fan letters from America with requests for posters and autographs. The only aspect of America that Sabbath did not like was the tougher attitude of the armed cops who attended rock festivals. Police were rarely if ever seen at British rock concerts or festivals, except for the occasional plain clothed drugs sleuth, but in the States they were hired to act as security, which seemed to provoke the crowds. Promoters feared the reaction of Sabbath crowds in particular. As the decade wore on, attitudes hardened and young people grew more violent. They had good cause to be nervous. But at the start of the Seventies Tony was adamant: 'I don't think playing loud and raw music makes the audience violent. The only

violence we get at shows is when we start it on stage! Sometimes the audience gets stirred up and that's great. We get excited on some numbers. I do a classical bit and if someone talks loudly I get annoyed and we all get annoyed, so the violence is just in us.'

There was some cause for celebration in May when the Royal Albert Hall relented on its Sabbath ban and the group played their first British concert in two months.

The group pleaded ignorance as to why the Albert Hall management had given into their demands to play, but there had probably been a bit of behind the scenes arm twisting from the Sabbath management.

'I don't know what prompted their decision. I think they must have just listened to our albums and decided the lyrics are true-to-life . . . I suppose we prick a few consciences in a way.' It was fascinating to imagine the respectable gentlemen of the Royal Albert Hall management sitting around a gramophone, winding it up, placing a Black Sabbath disc upon the turntable and silently sitting in judgement while Ozzy Osbourne screamed of *Children Of The Grave* and *War Pigs*.

'Hrrumph. Yes, most intriguing. I think this Mr. Osbourne has got something there. I can feel my conscience being pricked.'

In the event the concert was an orderly riot with 'new wave teenagers' as Disc magazine called them, 'screaming, shouting and clapping.' Interesting to note that 'head banger', 'skin head', and 'new wave' were all phrases well-worn before the advent of late Seventies punk or Eighties heavy metal.

The Albert Hall was the only gig Sabbath's UK fans could see for a while. The band were increasingly preoccupied with the vast army of enthusiasts waiting for them across the Atlantic. 'I was pleased with the American tour,' repeated Tony. 'I thought it went well for us except for one New York gig when we were tired and couldn't get into it. But in any case the kids don't rave *all* the time. We've still got a hard core of British fans and our records do well here, but I don't think we are being unfaithful.'

Nevertheless with advance orders of 200,000 for

their next LP giving them a tremendous boost to their confidence, they planned yet another six week American tour, from the temporary sanctuary of their Welsh cottage.

The lure of the country retreat appealed greatly to the men of the Midlands, who were driven west to escape the noise and smoke of the English cities. Now their sons needed to escape the clamour of their own doing, the thunder of a rock industry they had created, before it reduced them to quivering wrecks. Ozzy, always highly emotional, was in particular need of rest and recuperation, and from purely practical considerations, Sabbath could not be expected to write new material without a pause to recharge batteries.

Explained Tony: 'We decided we'd really have to get away from it all completely to get anything done. It's no good staying around home in Birmingham — I always end up in a club! We nearly accepted a one day gig in South Africa at the end of the May, just so we could take a week afterwards to write . . . but we'd have ended up sunbathing. We're a very lazy band!'

Once a band starts an upward curve it becomes increasingly difficult to stop working. They are driven on by the fear that it might all end tomorrow, by the need to maintain momentum and take advantage of higher fees for live performances, the offers of lucrative tours and expanding market for album sales. The band becomes a way of life for all those around it, the management, agents, promoters, road crews, technicians, and all the staff that work for them. Only one thing could stop Sabbath in its tracks towards the end of 1971, and that was illness.

In November it was announced that a forthcoming December British concert tour would have to be scrapped. Bill Ward was ill and could not go on the road. To make matters worse Ozzy was suffering from laryngitis. The voice, always so fragile, had not toughened up despite the long way the band had travelled from the German night clubs. The band had hoped to start 1972 with extensive touring, but no contracts could be signed.

But once again Christmas gave them the respite they needed and by January they fitted in a gig at Birmingham Town Hall, their old stamping ground. Said Ozzy: 'We haven't played here for such a long time I feel we've let down a lot of our loyal fans.' They set up a British tour eventually but there were no London dates this time.

Ozzy again: 'When we played at the Royal Albert Hall last year it was really emotional. We never enjoyed ourselves so much. The reason why the December tour was cancelled was because I was very ill when we returned from the States. I had a septic throat and temperature of 105 degrees. I was out of action for a month. As a result we had been pushed to get some new material for the act and its been hard work since.'

Their 1972 plans included the UK tour, four weeks in America in March and trips to Japan, Australia, New Zealand and anywhere else around the globe they could plug in and play. The fourth LP called *Black Sabbath Vol. 4* was to have been released in April and said the band 'The emphasis is on melody, while retaining Sabbath heaviness.'

Said Ozzy: 'This album has lots of short tracks for variety. Long numbers get boring. If we want to retain our popularity we will have to make a change. We're getting some weird effects in the studio, and doing insane things. For instance, we get everybody to march to the top of this big staircase the other day, singing like the Seven Dwarfs. It was amazing. Everybody let themselves go and we took it down on tape.'

By the end of the year, almost predictably the band were reported to be in a state of complete and utter exhaustion after several American tours. They were getting rich but they were risking their health and sanity.

The band kept going because they reasoned they had jumped so quickly into the success trap they didn't know how to get out. Ozzy thought long and hard about his situation. He knew something was seriously wrong but found it difficult to rationalise why musicians like them were prepared to undergo the pressures of hard touring when even the financial rewards could not compensate.

'Straight people probably say about us "To hell with them the idle bastards," but it's terrible man,' said Ozzy. 'Mentally it does you in. You end up drinking or take dope just to go on. I don't sleep properly. I haven't slept properly for months. It's getting worse all the time.' Sometimes Ozzy went without sleep for up to a week at a time, a deadly practice often followed by Keith Moon who was to pay the full price for non-stop Seventies-style raving. Ozzy was not hell bent on the same self-destructive cycle as Keith but he came pretty close. When he did get to sleep he often woke up shouting 'Hey, I'm on now!'

It got to the point where Ozzy thought he was going mad and went to see a psychiatrist. But he came away convinced that whatever was wrong with him, most psychiatrists were in a worse state, judging by some of the peculiar questions they asked. 'I believe I'm going nuts,' he confided in the summer of 1972. 'But so what? As long as I'm enjoying it.'

With the band in such a state there were the first hints that they might split up but they denied they were considering quitting. The dilemma was expressed in beautifully confused fashion by Ozzy: 'We want to stop touring. But I can't stop touring, 'cos I like it too much. Black Sabbath to me is my life,' he told Tony Stewart in an NME interview in 1972. 'This is what I've always wanted to do. It must have been, otherwise I couldn't have stuck it. We're the hardest working band around.'

There was no doubt the band still gained tremendous fun and excitement on the road in the States. The boring bits on airplanes, buses and in hotels were momentarily forgotten once they got on stage and felt the adrenalin flowing. One night during an endless tour they found themselves playing in a baseball stadium which had a high wire fence and several hundred yards of pitch separating audience from group. 'Come on inside' beckoned Ozzy who found it impossible to communicate with kids in such conditions.

Within seconds fans were climbing the fence and running towards the group in a human stampede. The band played on, intently watching the crowd that threatened to engulf them. But when they reached the stage, the kids didn't stop running. Instead they tramped right through the equipment and over the stage and rushed away across the field and out of the stadium doors. It was like a scene from a silent comedy, except for the racket the band and fans were making. And the reason for this mysterious behaviour? Hard on the heels of the fans, came the police!

Like most successful bands, Black Sabbath took on the services of a professional publicist. It was a tough job when reviews were consistently hostile. Keith Goodwin, who started out his career as a music journalist on the NME and then set up as an independent PR had handled a bizarre variety of artists over the years, from Dusty Springfield to Yes. But as a jazz and blues fan, he found much to identify with in Sabbath's music and admired their instrumental prowess.

'I always remember Tony Iommi saying to me "Nobody likes us – except the public." That became the band's stock phrase at a time when the reviewers didn't like 'em. But I liked their music, especially tunes like *Snowblind*. And I thought Bill Ward was a phenomenally good drummer. He could have walked into any band and played and there was a lot of jazz influence in his drumming. He was a great natural drummer but never got any credit for it. Of course the band played a very disciplined kind of music.'

'He had to play in a rigid, disciplined way, but to me Sabbath were the start of all the heavy metal bands, they were the kings of that style. Tony Iommi too was a much better guitarist than anybody gave him credit.'

Keith denies he ever concocted any 'black magic stories' about the group in their early days and says he doesn't even remember the subject being a topic for conversation except when they went to America. They had long feared that fans in the States would take their image too seriously and one night it came to the crunch. Ozzy walked out into the corridor of their hotel and found a group of fans holding black candles and standing in a circle. They were obviously hoping for a spot of fraternal devil worship with Sabbath in the sanctuary of their room. The band's roadie sprang to the rescue. He made the devotees of the black arts stand in a circle in their room, still clutching their candles. 'Now for the chant,' he said, raising arms in supplication. The roadie led the singing of 'Happy birthday to you . . .'

Although Goodwin had to be the purveyor of news about the group he often found himself battling against apathy or simple ignorance. 'I remember a certain journalist from a now defunct paper arriving to interview the band. Ozzy was going to do the interview while Tony was at a business meeting in the boardroom. The first question the bloke asked was "How many are there in the band?" Then he asked Ozzy: "What do you play?" The next thing I knew was Ozzy had walked out with a cry of "Fuck this" and had taken a cab home to Birmingham.'

When Goodwin did manage to get reporters together with the band, the usual questions were

about their excessive use of volume and how they got their sound.

Geezer was often the one called upon to explain Sabbath's musical philosophy. 'It's what our music demands,' he'd say. 'It's how we feel and how we write. Volume is an integral part of the music, which is rich, dark and sombre.'

Despite the sombre image, Keith was enamoured of his charges. 'I found them the four nicest blokes in rock. They were genuinely nice people — very bound up in their music. They came up with a new direction for rock. I think a lot of people had a secret love affair with Black Sabbath and wouldn't admit it.'

In September 1973 the band released what many have described as their masterpiece, the powerful *Sabbath, Bloody Sabbath*, inspired by the title of the Glenda Jackson/Peter Finch movie **Sunday Bloody Sunday**. The band may also have been nudged into using the title by a Melody Maker headline concocted by Alan Lewis, then an MM sub-editor and latterly editor of Sounds.

It was a year since their previous album *Volume 4* and Tony Iommi said that the band had planned to record in America, but surprisingly 'couldn't find a suitable studio.' They must have been feeling choosey, because America is almost wall-to-wall studios, with parking lots in between. But one of the LP's titles gave a clue to their real reason for their apparent tardiness. It was *Killing Yourself To Live*, and it summed up the group's feelings, as Tony said, 'after flogging around the States for the umpteenth time. We all started to fall over and get ill and that's why we have been out of action since December.

'It was just the travelling and the food. We were suffering from nervous exhaustion. We had been working solidly for three years. The last few months have given us time to take stock and think.'

The band was changing and Tony felt the slightly more malevolent aspects of their first two albums were being replaced by a more aggressive but less sinister approach.

Once again Tony looked back on the causes of their breakthrough four years earlier as if he still couldn't quite believe it had all happened.

'We were never really into black magic but we were the first of the really committed, loud and heavy bands,' he told NME's Keith Altham. 'We just decided to go all out and let go. It worked and we've stuck to that policy. In America they seem to think we have the same appeal as a horror movie. It's basically an act.'

This was the truth that many a would be sociologist refused to accept, not to mention the inevitable gaggle of sorcerers.

'I think volume is the key to most of the bad press we've had,' thought Tony. 'It's just that our generation of fans are used to that much more volume and like it. Critics are older — and don't. We've always kept our customers satisfied . . . and I personally believe in Sabbath.'

Tony could proudly point out that in 1973 the band could be compared in terms of drawing power and album sales with The Who and Led Zeppelin. 'But we seldom get recognition for it,' he said.

As the second half of the decade began, the band experienced a slow deterioration in the relationship between Ozzy and Tony Iommi and this was to have strange and wholly unexpected consequences for both group and singer. There would be many more alarms and excursions and personal tragedies. But nothing could take away their reputation and hard won riches, as the gold albums began to line up along the corridors of their stately homes.

CHAPTER 7
MUSICALLY SPEAKING-SABBATH

The conflicting forces of imagery and musical content can tear a band apart. They need both to survive, to project and clamour for the attention of the fickle masses. Black Sabbath's whole ethos could be explained away as cynical manipulation and commercialism, or simply as the work of untutored morons. This was the view frequently expostulated in the pages of such august journals as Rolling Stone, while British critics tended to flinch away from their efforts or simply poke fun.

I must admit my own reaction to Sabbath during their formative years was based largely on hearsay and prejudgements. When I met the band they proved to be pleasant, honest and open people without a trace of pretention, but with a stubborn desire to succeed that was perhaps more mystical than their flirtations with black magic. But later, as with so many other critics, I fell into the trap of ignoring the evidence of their own patently sincere endeavours, failed miserably to understand the appeal they had for a large section of rock fans, and bothered not to attempt to listen to their music with sufficient care and attention. It was too easy to erect barriers and take the safe, soft options.

Sabbath were loud on stage. Painfully loud. But not more so than the Who, or a vast array of volume bands from Vanilla Fudge onwards. I had survived close encounters with Blue Cheer, when they played at London's now defunct Revolution Club, and countless other gigs, including Grand Funk Railroad in Hyde Park and Ted Nugent in the sports arena in Phoenix, Arizona. Anyone who ventures near rock music must be prepared to have the ears blasted.

There were deeper, darker causes for hostility towards Sabbath. And I regret to say they had as much to do with prejudice as any serious musical objections. In my own case, I did not like their apparent dabblings in the occult. I'd been exposed to it already through contact with Graham Bond, a musician I greatly admired but became a great bore on the whole subject of 'holy magick.' Many had been the hours spent in pubs listening to Graham going on about the Tarot and forces of darkness, at once lecturing and attempting to convert me to the black priesthood. All I really needed to know about was the title of the next album.

Thus I had a built in hostility to something that I

could see was real enough — in the eyes of the committed — and if the truth were known, probably could lead to all kinds of death and disaster. My instinctive gut reaction to the whole subject was to leave it well alone, and that no good could come of it. Indeed all the people I knew in the Sixties who became involved in magic ended up dead, ill or demented, while their careers reached unnatural heights and then plummetted with sickening force.

My early encounters with Sabbath should have shown me that they were using imagery for publicity and as soon as the *Black Sabbath* album was released, they were busy denying they had any serious connections with the occult. But there were other causes of prejudice, apparent in retrospect. They were working class lads from Birmingham, not smart, well spoken, highly educated boys from the Home Counties. Their earthiness and simplicity made them the butt of jokes and satire. At the MM we used to imagine someone of the stature of John Freeman or Ludovic Kennedy interviewing the group on TV: 'Tell me Geezer . . .'

The fact that kids in their thousands, the very readers whose opinions we fondly imagined had their views shaped by our ceaseless flow of comment and advice, were turning their backs on 'the good' and were heading hotfoot for the bad and the ugly, was a saluatory lesson in humility for rock journalists.

It was convenient to fall for the line that Sabbath 'couldn't play' that they had no talent, and relied solely on the most basic, primitive riffs. Even supporters of the band liked to perpetuate the belief that Bill Ward was only capable of bashing out an off-beat with the minimal technique and that Ozzy was little more than a bellowing animal. The band were only too aware of this hostility that bordered on contempt, and this caused Tony Iommi to over compensate, playing those celebrated 15 minute guitar solos which he only abandoned in the Eighties, after Ozzy had left.

But were Sabbath ever such a basic, uncouth band? Were they musical anarchists, out to destroy the whole complex progress of rock's musical advancement? Strangely enough, Sabbath themselves have always seen themselves on a pathway of musical progress, and it was only towards the end that Ozzy claimed he wanted a return to simplicity. But even good old simplistic rock'n'roll requires a high degree of musical skill for it to be performed adequately and with conviction.

Strip away the horror stories, the imagery and hysteria, turn down the amps a notch, and you have a well rehearsed, solid blues and rock band, powered by a dedication to well defined objectives. A band *different* from predecessors like the Yardbirds, Cream and Hendrix, and contemporaries like Led Zeppelin and Deep Purple but in many ways just as good. And the evidence lies in their recorded out-put, in particular their early albums and singles. The first album *Black Sabbath* was made at a cost of £600

in a couple of days in a London studio, but it captured the spirit of the band in a way that much more expensive and time consuming projects can rarely achieve.

The records stand up well some twelve years later, and played along side many albums of the period, positively shine forth with the brilliance and authority of their attack. Black Widow, the much vaunted black magic band of the period who were frequently confused with Sabbath sound quite feeble, particularly in the rhythm section. Even Cream and Blind Faith could not match Sabbath for the 'live' excitement and presence that permeated that first effort and only Led Zeppelin's first album could match them for power.

Apart from the stunning introduction with its teaming rain, church bells and thunder, the original *Black Sabbath* track teaches us that Ozzy Osbourne had a voice of such quality and unique flavour it could only be the work of an original talent. Maybe there is something in the water around the Birmingham area that affects the vocal chords but there was a pained, swallowing in Ozzy's voice that in retrospect reminds me of Steve Winwood.

The stalking Iommi guitar and tumbling, muffled drums of Bill Ward all contributed in sophisticated fashion to this remarkable performance, a tone poem of a type rarely achieved in all the 25 years history of rock. There was an element of tongue-in-cheek humour in Ozzy's vocal *tour de force*, but you have to search hard to find it. As master of the 'wind up' never was his acting ability put to a greater test than on this gothic horror story which gave the band it's character, for better or worse, for the ensuing decade.

The blues roots and flexibility of Sabbath was best revealed on another great performance, *The Wizard*, an arrangement full of twisting ideas and imaginative interplay.

The Wizard remains one of my all-time favourite Sabbath cuts, with its train whistle call from Ozzy's harmonica leading the way into a real Sixties R&B burn up. As Tony's guitar bubbles and boils, Bill Ward has to pick his way through a mine field of

changes in beat, tempo and a series of gaps in the barbed wire which he has to fill with tricky snare, tom tom and bass drums beats that compared well with the work of his compatriot John Bonham. Bill, if anything, had a slightly lighter touch than John and was capable of 'filling-in' with all the panache of a jazz big band drummer. It is this jazzy feel which belies the myth of Sabbath as a mindless heavy metal machine. The unison riff of Butler and Iommi sounded fierce and menacing and was played with a driving fury that seemed shocking by the standards of 1970.

The blues and not metal permeated other performances of the era like *Warning* and for an untaught singer, raised on a childhood love for the Beatles (he wanted to be Paul McCartney), Ozzy showed impressive mastery in the art of delivering a lyric imbued with meaning.

Whence came Ozzy's vocal experience if, as he claimed, he leapt straight from prison into the arms of Earth? There is no doubt he had earlier brushes with the vocal art which lent him encouragement. He once said his first gig was singing at a wedding held at Salisbury fire station in 1965, with a band called The Music Machine. Later on he recorded with a band called Magic Lanterns which made two albums and one single. Discographers have unearthed the albums called *Shame Shame* on the Atlantic label (SD8217) and *Lit Up With The Magic Lanterns*. The titles alone hint at a mixture of flower power and soul, the two prevailing influences during the middle Sixties. And that might explain Ozzy's later contempt for the hippie movement. Incidentally research has also shown that in 1967 Ozzy and Geezer were in a band called Rare Breed while Bill Ward and Tony Iommi were in another obscure outfit – Mythology. When both bands split, Ozzy, Geezer, Bill and Tony formed Earth.

There is nothing like a series of duff groups to spur a man on to develop his own style. And the Osbourne voice emerged drenched in pain, frustration, anger, self-torment and black humour. Just the conditions brought on by rehearsals with bands sans gigs, sans money, sans everything.

Even Earth could not fully provide the escape route to oblivion and fulfilment these repressed teenagers desired. Tony Iommi put it in more practical terms. 'We couldn't keep playing 12-bars for ever. We just got fed up with Earth music. It was jazz, blues stuff. It was good for practice but nothing else. A lot of other groups were playing the same thing. When we changed the whole thing just snowballed. We wanted something of our own that we'd like and people would like. And we wanted something loud!'

And by Jove they got it. Strangely enough mere volume does not enter the argument when probing Sabbath on record.

There is a cunning volume control invariably fitted to modern electric gramophones that reduces the decibel level of the most obdurately noisy rhythm combo. And while Tony may have pooh-poohed their jazz roots there is no doubt early Sabbath music SWUNG more than it ROCKED. It was a characteristic they should have pursued rather than discarded.

Certainly *The Wizard* has swing and is loaded with the use of dynamic phrasing that is far removed from the mechanical bludgeoning of most heavy metal. Listening afresh to performances like this, it is all the more extraordinary that Rolling Stone could call their music 'a cynical murky drone.' Perhaps they were thinking of *Warning* a piece that emanated from the highly respected Aynsley Dunbar's Retaliation and was 'covered' on the *Black Sabbath* album. There is nothing moronic or stupid about Iommi's simple, direct guitar on a well crafted model solo. Thwarted somewhat in their intentions by the indifferent 'boomy' studio sound, nevertheless the different segments of the arrangement built up the kind of tension and excitement that had been whipping up hysteria among Sabbath's fans in clubs and pubs. All this particular recording needed to complete the authentic atmosphere of the times was the sound of beer crates being stacked and the distant yelp of the crowd.

Iommi's guitar work may have become overstretched at times, but on this performance of *Warning* his playing has a sense of purpose and intuitive understanding of the value of space between the onslaught of notes. The band also had that sense of fair play that stems from the jazz jam session tradition. It's unlikely they thought of it in those terms, but it certainly enabled Geezer, for example, to start off a *N.I.B.* with an angry, thrumming bass solo, a freedom that would be frowned upon by today's producers. (Indeed the solo was cut out of later re-issues).

It is not stretching the point too much to say that there are moments during the creation of *Black Sabbath* (the album), when the band begin to sound like the Mahavishnu Orchestra in full cry. Certainly the blue of guitar lines and cymbal and drum thunder at the climax of *N.I.B.* has the same sort of liberation enjoyed by John McLaughlin and Billy Cobham. But perhaps the performance that is most far removed from the image of Sabbath-as-bozos is *Wicked World* the B-side to their first single *Evil Woman* released January and March of 1970. Bill Ward kicks off with a 'sighing hi-hat' of the kind favoured by Jo Jones and Tony snaps in with an impudent and cutting riff, rounded off by Bill's drums that fade then return with abrupt, fierce snare drum accents. It's all a build up for Ozzy's stunning vocals over a craggy, mountainous backbeat. A cerebral Iommi guitar rumination is interrupted by a return to the snazzy, jazzy theme that started it all. And all this was dumped on a B side.

Paranoid the title track of the second album, released in September 1970, is a folk song of roundelay construction and indeed Ozzy instinctively sings it in minstrel style. He laments the parting of ways with his wench who proved something of a failure in providing comfort, solace and understanding. The original 'cry for help' it says more about the problems of youth than many a TV documentary, and of course it tells us a lot about Ozzy's own psychological disorders.

With Bill's drums chopping the riff into manageable chunks, and bass and guitar locked in deadly embrace, the whole thing is a *chef d'oeuvre*. Ozzy suffered on earlier recordings by having his voice buried in the track. But he bellowed forth loud and clear on the piece many believe represents Sabbath's finest hour, the remarkable *War Pigs*.

At the time of its release it caused a furore. Many hated its doomy sentiments, coming hard on the heels of the psychedelic dream. The Vietnam war was raging and many youngsters now refused to believe all could be cured by an exchange of flowers and a browse through Tolkien.

Ozzy painted a black picture of war and evil – an Hieronymus Bosch painting in sound. As with all Sabbath performances of the period it was no mere 32-bar song with a catchy hook, but an elaborate imaginative arrangement which stretched the ability of the whole band. Ozzy once told how *War Pigs* was all about 'VIPS sitting there saying "Go out and fight" and all the every-day people being forced to. We're not a political group. It's just that most of our songs have a message.'

Many stumbling on *War Pigs* for the first time, with its eerie siren and reminders of the Blitz could be forgiven for feeling shocked and rejecting such alien music. And there was more to come when the band bored deeper into gloomy presentiments with the astonishing *Iron Man* which can now be seen as a precursor of much of today's sci-fi pop. On this cut Sabbath sound remarkably close to King Crimson who had released their *In The Court Of The Crimson King* album in 1969, and created a stir with their *21st Century Schizoid Man*. It is unlikely that *Iron Man* was conceived as a tribute to Crimson but merely reflected the range of possible directions the band were exploring during those heady days of rock experiment.

Fairies Wear Boots also from *Paranoid* showed the mighty Bill Ward at his most flexible and once again displayed the band's penchant for changing the mood of a piece in drastic fashion after a couple of choruses, of which modern HM bands seem incapable. 'Going home late last night, suddenly I got a fright,' sang Ozzy. He saw 'fairies in boots' often interpreted as a satirical poke against skinheads. Ozzy put it down to hallucinations. He also explained that *Iron Man* was 'about a guy who invents a time machine and finds the world is coming to an end. He comes back and turns to iron and people won't listen to him.'

'They think he's not real. He goes a bit barmy and decides to get his revenge by killing people. He tries to do good but in the end it turns into bad.'

Other tracks like *Electric Funeral* were about the possibility of a nuclear war and *Hand Of Doom* was

about drug addiction. 'If you can frighten people with words, it's better than letting them find out by trying drugs,' said Ozzy. Despite the violent and oppressive nature of the work it was actually rehearsed in the pleasant surroundings of a small studio on a farm in rural Wales and the rough takes were also recorded there.

The lyrics to all Sabbath songs were written in direct couplets that enabled Ozzy to deliver them with maximum power and effect. There should have been no room for misinterpretations, but it was an age when hidden meanings were sought in everything from Stonehenge to the cover of the Beatles' *Abbey Road* album. Sabbath words were inevitably placed under close scrutiny and hotly debated.

Commented Tony: 'One of the biggest problems with the music scene is the kids try and read things into songs. They try and interpret lyrics and often create things that aren't there. Our music is simple, basic stuff, the lyrics are plain, laid on a plate – you can't misunderstand them. *War Pigs* and the drug songs are just our opinions. We're not trying to influence people. We don't know if people take it all in.'

They probably sucked in *Sweet Leaf*, the opening cut of their 1971 album *Master Of Reality*. Just in case there was any doubt in the minds of the audience, Ozzy emitted a racking cough before launching into a pæan of praise for the pleasures of the weed. 'Straight people don't know what you're about. They put you down and shut you out. You gave me a new belief. And soon the world will love you sweet leaf,' sang Ozzy. The song was obviously about tea.

The sound of the album was smooth and lacked the echoing power that characterised earlier productions. Bill's drums had the muffled sound favoured by engineers who were forever ruining the tone of drums by covering them with sticky tape and inserting travelling rugs, carpets, bedspreads, pillows and cushions inside bass drums. Thus an otherwise pokey tune, *After Forever* lacks any kind of presence. Surprisingly, in view of Sabbath's image, this is a song that calls for others to follow Ozzy's lead and accept the teachings of the Lord. He says with great fervour: 'I have seen the truth. Yes I have seen the light and I've changed my ways. And I'll be prepared when you're lonely and scared at the end of our days.' If Ozzy was really talking about himself, an element of wishful thinking had crept in.

Master Of Reality had marching, doom laden items like *Children Of The Grave* and some attractive instrumental passages, including an acoustic guitar ditty, *Orchid*. But the overall production was flat and pulled the punches of *Lord Of This World* and the guitar and bass riffs began to sound dangerously monotonous rather than dramatic. *Into The Void* had good science fiction lyrics about rockets and the end of Mankind (as we know it) which Ozzy delivered with his usual menace. But the pace had slackened, the element of surprise faded.

Even hard core Sabbath fans began to wonder if the band was losing its grip.

Then the dust and fug of *Master* was swept away with the arrival of *Black Sabbath Volume 4* in September 1972. Made at The Record Plant, in Los Angeles, American technology enabled Vic Smith to capture Sabbath to best advantage. From the opening bars of *Wheels Of Confusion* a roaring clarity prevailed. Bill's drums thrashed with unfettered power, played with the kind of fervour one might expect from Keith Moon. And once again the guitars rang forth with bold confidence.

Tony was in inspired mood and soloed with sustained improvisational brilliance. But the greatest moment on this *tour de force* was reserved for Ozzy who stunned Sabbath fans with his interpretation of *Changes*. One of the band's most melodic and attractive songs it was issued as a B side to *Sabbath Bloody Sabbath* in single form but should have been an international hit. Ozzy poured his soul into the lyrics with heartfelt concern and created a work that could easily match Robert Plant's *Stairway To Heaven*. The piano accompaniment was perfect, although slightly spoilt by a Mellotron attempting to give a somewhat banal string effect.

The band then roared through *Supernaut* on all six cylinders and on the precise and kicking *Snowblind* (a slightly slower, distant cousin of *Paranoid*), dispelled all rumours and fears about the future of Sabbath music. Another highlight of the album was the rotary riff of *Under The Sun* complete with gong crescendo and double tracked guitar lines.

A year later came their fifth album which many felt was their finest to date, the celebrated *Sabbath Bloody Sabbath*, which included tracks that were destined to become firm favourites and the staple diet of future tours, like *Sabbra Cadabra*, *Killing Yourself To Live* and *Spiral Architect*.

The title track is another vocal triumph for Ozzy, following in the wake but in an entirely different style from *Changes*.

Sabbath Bloody Sabbath was full of surprises and hidden pleasures. Apart from the ferociously heavy main riff, on which bass and lead guitar seem to melt together from the heat, there is a 'middle eight' section where Wes Montgomery style guitars interweave behind Ozzy's relaxed vocal which gives way to the unexpected but wholly convincing cry of 'You bastards!' You can almost see Ozzy the prisoner peering through the prison bars and shouting at the screws. The lyrics can be interpreted in many ways, as an attack on cant and hypocrisy and more directly as a rebuff of those incessant critical snipes against the band. 'Living just for dying, dying just for you!' roars Ozzy just before Tony's guitar peels off to attack like a Spitfire in a dogfight.

Sabbath kept up a remarkably high standard of production throughout their career with Ozzy in terms of new songs, new ideas and treatments. Take *Am I Going Insane?* for example, from their 1975 LP

Sabotage. A bolero drum beat surges forwards beneath Ozzy's mysteriously electronic vocal track. The mood recalls the Who in their *I Can See For Miles* period, and concludes with some rather maniacal laughter that is exceedingly disturbing, especially if heard on headphones.

And so the work of recording, writing and performing went on via such albums as *Technical Ecstasy*, hailed at the time as a major breakthrough for the band in its incessant search for new directions, and *Never Say Die* released in 1978. But then came the great shake ups in the band and *Heaven And Hell* appeared in 1980, marking the arrival in the ranks of American singer Ronnie James Dio. Bill Ward remained on drums, together with the old firm of Iommi and Butler. It was produced and engineered by Martin Birch and extra keyboards were added by Geoff Nicholls.

'Good things never last' sang Ronnie on his debut tune *Neon Knights*. Certainly the days of sound poems and social documentaries were over, but this was a new slicker Sabbath, closer in spirit to the Heavy Metal Revival that had overtaken the original bands of the late Sixties. Sabbath came out fighting, proving that when it came to fast tempos, a rock solid beat and flurries of smoking guitar notes, nobody was going to outgun Sabbath. There was no doubt some of the magic had gone, the unpredictable flavour that Ozzy's presence naturally engendered. But on *Neon Knights* it was hard to believe this was a band who had been ensconced in studios for some ten years. They sounded as fresh and committed as ever, and Ronnie's voice had all the adaptibility that befitted someone who had spent time teaching singing. In tunes like *Children Of The Sea* he showed he could tackle a ballad with technical expertise and impressive zeal. Older Sabbath fans mourned the passing of Ozzy's inner torment that made each song a Shakespearian tragedy.

Bill's drums had lost none of their power over the years, and whereas he had been more prone to experiment in days of yore, his bass drum still kicked like a mule and he'd throw in ideas to break up the relentless beat demanded of rhythm sections in the new decade. And Tony's guitar had never been better recorded than it was on *Heaven And Hell*. Strangely enough his riff on *Lady Evil* bore a close resemblance to Cliff Richard's hit *Devil Woman*. When one considers devils, women and evil, the same thoughts tend to spring to mind. And also it has to be said that title track commits the unforgivable sin of being boring, something Sabbath had never been throughout their career. They made up for it with more active and sprightly tunes like *Wishing Well*. On *Die Young* with the keyboards and vocal harmonies, the band begin to sound like their old touring partners Yes, circa 1970. And when they get back into the hard rocking, with Geezer's bass working overtime, they more than make up for *Heaven And Hell* with one of their most driving performances on record.

By the time Bill Ward left to be replaced by Vinnie Appice, Black Sabbath were a new band, and once again they went into the studios with producer Martin Birch to come up with their October 1981 offering *Mob Rules* complete with suitably terrifying cover of a scaffold and hooded proletarian seekers of vengeance. The band went back to The Record Plant to make the record which did not differ noticeably in sound quality from *Heaven And Hell* except that Vinnie obtained greater ride cymbal clarity – not something to concern the average head banger. The overall effect was of a power rock band out to get audiences on their feet and cheering such items as *Falling Off The Edge Of The World*. With less emphasis on atmosphere and messages and more on efficient use of energy, the result was a competent, modern album but largely lacking in the spark of inspiration that had distinguished the band throughout its career. Perhaps musicians need uncertainty and tension to bring out the best, and reliable teamwork, as Orson Welles tells us in **The Third Man** simply results in the predictability of 'the cuckoo clock.'

The lyrics too lacked the concern and naive confusion of youth and most importantly – English working class youth, that distinguished Sabbath at their best. Songs like *The Sign Of The Southern Cross* were more the product of grown men, grown used to living an up market existence, much of it in America far from the pie stalls of their native heath. It would be ridiculous to expect them to relate to their youth for ever and for Sabbath to continue to rail against a world that had as the Scottish trade unionists say 'at the end of the day' been good to them.

The average Birmingham lad, dodging the muggers, litter and graffiti 'twixt the battered safety railings around the thruways and underpasses, could no more relate to *The Sign Of The Southern Cross* than an LA millionaire could relate to *Sabbath Bloody Sabbath*. But *Mob Rules* was a bow in the direction of the masses, closer to the 'Get down all you beasts' ethos of Saxon, Krokus, Iron Maiden and their ilk. Certainly the new boys tore into their work with enthusiasm, with Vinnie's drumming closely resembling his older brother Carmine's heavy use of tom toms and a big authorative bass drum, notably on *Slipping Away*. Ronnie delivered the lyrics, even of the 'I think I'm losing my mind' variety, with a smooth sophistication on *Falling Off The Edge Of The World*, a piece which harked back to original Sabbath ideals.

In the midst of all this revamping there appeared in June 1980 a testament to the original group, *Live At Last* consisting of 'live' performances culled from gigs at the Rainbow, London and in Manchester. It featured the old firm of Ozzy, Iommi, Ward and Butler, and showed them hard at work on familiar material *Sweet Leaf*, *Killing Yourself To Live*, *Snowblind*, *War Pigs*, *Wicked World* and *Paranoid*.

The group were unhappy at its release, and were probably aware of all the flaws and fluffs inevitable

in the cut and thrust of a live gig. But the sound quality is good, Ozzy sings well and you can hear that the audience is certainly having a good time. And to many ears it is preferable to and more entertaining than *Heaven And Hell* for all the latter's technical perfection.

After the Osbourne departure, Ozzy wasted no time in putting his own band together and released his first album *Blizzard Of Ozz* in September 1980 with Randy Rhoads (guitars), Bob Daisley (bass), and Lee Kerslake (drums). They launched into the first track *Don't Know* with tremendous verve and Ozzy instantly showed that he had a lot more to say and that he had not been drained by his years with Sabbath. A revealing back cover picture showed that the youthful innocence of 1968 had faded to be replaced by sad eyes and an expression that hinted at infinite sadness within the Osbourne soul, often the way with clowns. But the Osbourne spirit was high and a touch of bathos evident in the small matter of Ozzy having forgotten to tuck his shirt in while posing in sombre mood for the camera. Randy made a tremendous contribution to the success of this album and its follow up *Diary Of A Madman* which both serve as fine memorials in the light of his tragic death in a 'plane crash.

On *Madman* the music was given a huge shot in the arm by the addition of powerhouse Tommy Aldridge on drums who made a more noticeable contribution than Vinnie Appice made to Sabbath's *Mob Rules*. From the launch of *Over The Mountain* Tommy's drums make *Madman* a much more attacking album, and Randy is obviously inspired by the percussive crossfire.

The themes are inevitably self-obsessed and concerned with suicide, psychotic disorders, sexual hang ups, and our old friend black magic. Just the right mixture to send American teenagers into paroxysms of delight. And with the latter album in particular Ozzy became everybody's Halloween trick or treat. He appears on the cover in a bloodstained travesty of the bird suit he wore on *Black Sabbath Volume 4*. Crosses abound on both covers but the prophecies of doom that characterised Sabbath in their classic period seem closer at hand and of a personal nature. Robots and nuclear war are replaced by the trapped prisoner of guilt and fear. Randy Rhoads co-produced *Madman* with Ozzy and engineer Max Norman, and the result was a stunning rock'n'roll statement peppered with delights like the tale of voodoo *Little Dolls* and the hard hitting *S.A.T.O.* notable for some of Randy's most furious guitaring. For the first time Ozzy's voice was in danger of being pushed aside by these instrumental young lions, in a way that even years of Sabbath at maximum power had not managed.

But he reasserted all his character and spine tingling touches of evil and possession on the moving *Diary Of A Madman* one of his most passionate performances since the days of *Changes*.

Both Sabbath and Ozzy were able to pursue their own paths and ideas after the split with a greater freedom perhaps than the old strictures of tradition allowed.

And perhaps there isn't that much of a difference between *Black Sabbath* in 1970 and *Diary Of A Madman* in 1981. The power — and the madness — remain the same.

CHAPTER 8
NEVER SAY DIE

By 1974 Black Sabbath were part of the World Wide Artists management company run by Patrick Meehan, and their records including *Sabbath Bloody Sabbath* and reissues of earlier Sabbath albums and singles were released on their WWA label. The company's product was handled by the much larger Phonogram company. Also in the stable of talent were the Groundhogs, Gentle Giant and Medicine Head. Wilf Pine operated from an office in London's Dover Street where he looked after the affairs of Stray and the Groundhogs.

The life styles of the two partners was markedly different. Wilf, one time bouncer on the Isle Of Wight, had 'love' and 'hate' tattooed on his hand and could be seen enjoying his leisure hours in the various music business niteries. Patrick preferred the life of a successful but hip entrepreneur and loved to escape to his yacht moored off Cannes. Patrick was feted in the press as a 25-year-old multi-millionaire who it was claimed, owned several luxury homes including a £200,000 16th century stately mansion in Kent, eight cars and the celebrated yacht.

It was said that only six years earlier he had been a £4.50 a week articled clerk with a city firm of chartered accountants, living at home with his parents in the suburbs. The music business seemed an attractive way to make money and use his accounting skills. Within three years he pushed World Wide Artists, which started with £27 capital, from a small agency to a big time operation which cost Equity Enterprises a 'seven figure sum' when they took it over and made Meehan a director.

Despite the success and opulence all was not well behind the scenes. There were arguments about money and a feeling of dissatisfaction which eventually led Black Sabbath to break away from the whizz kid management team in 1975. They tried to manage themselves but this proved more irksome than they imagined and eventually took on Mark Forster and Albert Chapman to look after them.

The mid-Seventies were marked by tax and management problems that weighed them down. The band began to gain a reputation for being 'difficult' as they failed to turn up for interviews and reacted in confused and irritated fashion. Ozzy seemed wilder than ever and was frequently ill. Typically he responded to their crisis by writing a

song on their 1975 *Sabotage* album called *Am I Going Insane?* These pressures did not help their inter-band relationships. Ozzy developed a penchant for ripping up the bibles placed in American hotels 'by the Gideons' an act of destruction which incensed Tony Iommi who eventually punched Ozzy on the nose.

In March 1976 Jim Simpson's case against the group and their managers, was heard in the High Court in London. Jim, then aged 38, was seeking damages for alleged breach of contract by Sabbath and charged that 'the fruits of efforts in steering Black Sabbath had been filched.' Jim was eventually awarded his damages but had a long wait for the money. In the aftermath the group were determined to sort out their affairs once and for all, and began to claw back and enjoy money the band had generated. Big cars and big houses were theirs at last, without any fear of their being repossessed.

And throughout it all Sabbath knew one force in the land they could rely on and trust. 'The fans keep us alive,' said Geezer Butler in January 1976. 'We have been knocked by the critics but the fans have stayed loyal. And the numbers are growing all the time.'

'We've had to become businessmen, through no choice of our own,' said Tony. 'But playing to the people, all along, came first.'

Settlement was reached with Jim Simpson and by that time they had severed all managerial contracts and decided to try and handle all their own business, even if they needed day-to-day management help, from Albert Chapman.

'The effect of all this has been very tiring,' said Ozzy later. 'It separated us from what we were here for. We were more tied up sitting in solicitors' offices than in getting things together as a band. I just didn't want to know anything about that. I wanted to get it out of my head.' He claimed that the form of madness he was suffering had been caused by the pressures and his disillusionment with the entire music business. Ozzy took out his frustrations by shooting, often at windows, but never, he protested, at cats, as has been rumoured. 'Oh no, I've never shot a cat!' he said. 'I once shot a horse. It's just that I dig shooting. I've got guns in the house.' Long walks in the countryside with his dog and guns helped ease the tension whenever he thought about all those lawyers, solicitors and managers squabbling over his earnings.

During 1974 and 1975 the band had enjoyed sell-out tours of America. There was no danger of their appeal slipping, whatever the internal problems they might be suffering. In July 1975 they released the *Sabotage* album after a long gestation period, and celebrated this with their first appearance at Madison Square Garden. In October they toured Britain and Europe, with concerts at Glasgow, London and Birmingham. The response was heart warming. If Sabbath had ever been reduced to tears by their management and courtroom battles, they must have shed more with emotion at the scenes they witnessed. Legions of headbangers strummed imaginary guitars and cardboard replicas. Ozzy joined in and toted his own imaginary guitar. Tony, resplendent in his white satin costume with gold braid and long sleeves didn't seem to mind these mass immitations.

Ozzy was such a star. His wife Thelma lovingly created a wardrobe of costumes in red, yellow or white with leather tassles and matching stack heel boots.

Night after night Ozzy poured out his soul on stage, giving those famous peace signs. How did all that start? 'I just did it to them one day – and they all did it back!'

The peace sign had an added irony in view of the violence that seemed to permeate Sabbath music and audience response, particularly in America. Crossed fingers might have been more appropriate. But there was something lovable about Ozzy's confusion, his sincerity and the ever present 'manic compulsiveness' that continued to land him in fat, fire and boiling water throughout his career.

In October 1975 when the band had first decided to manage itself as a kind of co-operative, they reached the decision they would have to leave Britain because of the then Labour Government's high rate of taxation. Chancellor Denis Healey had become rock's bogey man causing a mass emigration of rock stars who didn't mind earning dollars for their country, but didn't want to give it all away. 'It's a very sad thing for me that we have to leave England,' he told MM's Harry Doherty. 'Because of the state of the economics of this country we're being forced to go. We cannot afford to function under these tax things so we'll have to join all the rest and wave bye-bye.' Ozzy thought the Government was forcing all the talent out of the country and there was no doubt he had a point, although such complaints by successful rock stars were among the roots causes of the Punk Rock revolution just about to explode.

Ozzy had an answer for the critics. 'It must sound as if everybody in the rock business is tight and they don't want to share the money, but it's not like that. People in the business have a limited amount of time. You're only young once and I can't be doing Black Sabbath when I'm 58. I don't expect to be the wild kid from Aston when I'm that age.'

'I don't want to be wealthy for the rest of my life. I want to be comfortable. I want to sit and dedicate myself to music in whatever way it comes out, but with all these tax laws, at the age of 38 we'll probably all have to sign back on the dole again. I don't think we deserve that.

'Each of us has worked bloody hard for whatever we've got. I wish a lot of people would try and get that sunk in their heads a bit. It's fun but you have a lot of hang-ups, a lot of mental hang-ups, a lot of physical hang-ups.'

Ozzy didn't know where he was going to go but thought he might check out China or become a gypsy and live in a tent. One thing was certain, he claimed he didn't want to be a country squire for the rest of his life, so often the life style chosen by the *nouveau riche* of rock. Ozzy rejected the idea of going to live in America because he claimed that he was frightened by the escalating urban violence which was beginning to affect rock concerts.

'It just freaks me out man. You go on stage and see 15 people in the circle battering each other to pieces. We're still gotta try and say "We love you"; with this guy lying on the floor with a bottle sticking out of his throat. That's one thing everybody has got to understand about Black Sabbath's lyrics. They're not downer lyrics, they're just telling everybody where it's at. That's all it is. People must think we sleep off the rafters with wings on our backs every night, taking reds and drinking wine. We're just people.

'We see a lot and we write about what we see. We have a couple of songs about people getting stoned but so have a lot of people. It's a heavy, doomy thing but it's what we see. Love wouldn't go with the style of music we play. It would be like going to see Frankenstein with the Sound Of Music soundtrack behind it.'

Ozzy explained: 'The way we write goes with the way be play. We're not telling everybody to jump off the cliff and if anybody ever did, I don't know what I'd do. If that happened I'd believe I was the devil.'

Despite their endless protestations that they were essentially non-violent people, it was still obvious that Sabbath's music caused kids to over-react. Said Ozzy: 'If people can come to a Black Sabbath gig or listen to a Black Sabbath record and get rid of their aggressions, that's great. If they're miserable they can put on a Black Sabbath record and think that the band knows how they feel. They've got something they can relate to. It's great to see kids at our gigs enjoying themselves and not kicking shit out of each other.'

Ozzy confirmed that being in the band had been one of the great experiences of his life and in the wake of the *Sabotage* album he thought they were all stronger musicians capable of considerable progression. He felt they had been changing gradually since their inception and had always avoided taking the gamble of too drastic a change in their music and image. They had fought hard for their success and were not about to throw it all away with some musical gamble that fans might reject. It took them a year to make *Sabotage* and Ozzy felt this was too long. He discussed the project with typical humour.

'In the end I felt like calling it Crossroads. Everytime there was a session we used to call it Chapter 99 – "Will Black Sabbath complete the album this time?"' The making of the album seemed like a nightmare enlivened only on the night they started throwing custard pies at each other in the studio.

Ozzy hated *Sabotage* on first hearing but later realised this was a reaction to weeks of living with the same music. 'It's not that bad considering we were all going through a lot of hassles with our own heads, like "Where can we go from here? What are we going to do to be better than the last one?" To me *Sabotage* beats the last album but I still like that one.'

Ozzy thought long and hard about his position as a rock idol with an army of admirers. 'It's good because I've made people happy. People are getting high off it. If people want to idolise me, they can. That's what I'm in it for. That's my job. I really dig making people happy and that's genuine.'

He was less certain about the benefits of big money. 'We've had a bit of extra money but I think that money is pretty evil. Sure you need it to survive but it's brought me a lot of unhappiness. Through wealth you lose much of your identity and you don't communicate with people. Not the way you could before.'

Ozzy experienced the bitter alienation from friends that money can bring. 'Your old friends look on you as if you are not there,' said Ozzy sadly. 'I just want to keep as many of my old friends as possible but you can't always do that. They change their attitude towards you.'

Ozzy had discovered the paradox of wealth and easy living. One yearned for it from teenage years onwards and then found it caused more problems than it solved. But then Ozzy always had a confused relationship with the world, and was prone to jumping in and trying anything at least once, usually with disastrous results. Before he became a rock star (a role he carved for himself with great panache and success), he was tempted by a life of crime. For Ozzy, as with most things, it seemed like a good idea at the time. And for a while at least, he enjoyed the excitement it offered and the camaraderie – even in prison where he eventually wound up.

'When I was in nick, I never remembered the downers, only the good laughs we had sometimes,' reminisced Ozzy at the height of his success with Sabbath. 'But I wouldn't like to go back there again. I like my freedom.'

Ozzy was charged with Grand Larceny and was in Winson Green prison near Birmingham for two months back in 1967. On one occasion he stole a television set and was found balanced on top of a wall that had been unfairly lined with slivers of glass, to prevent just such persons as John Osbourne from making off. He fell off the wall and landed with the 24 inch TV set on his chest. Ozzy's screams pierced the night air.

Once inside prison his biggest complaint was boredom. 'I had nothing to do inside. You did about two hours work a day and the rest of the time you were locked in your cell. That's when I did my tattoos – with a sewing needle and tins of grate polish.' So why had Ozzy turned to singing? 'When I came out of nick . . . I had to do something didn't I?'

If Ozzy was confused by the wealth that could have bought him a warehouse full of 24 inch TV sets, the rest of the band had few problems adapting. Bill Ward and Melinda bought a farm in Worcestershire and settled down, in much the same fashion as his contemporary, drummer and farmer John Bonham in Led Zeppelin. Ozzy had a ranch style home in Staffordshire while Geezer lived in what was described as 'solitary confinement' on acres of Worcestershire woodland.

Tony Iommi had moved up in the world with a vengeance. His wife Susan was related to royal photographer Lord Snowden and they lived on 44 acres in Leicestershire. As if Sabbath affairs were not enough he also expanded his business interests into looking after such bands as Budgie and Judas Priest through an agency run with a friend.

Tony was the proud owner of a Lamborghini or two, and a Rolls Royce, appropriate status symbols for a man who scuffled his way up through the stews of rock and roll. Incidentally Sabbath were once thus described by Ken Tucker of the Los Angeles Herald Examiner: 'Would be English Kings of Heavy Metal . . . eternally foiled by their stupidity and intractability.' Tony could ponder such accusations of stupidity while splashing in the swimming pool or enjoying a game of tennis on his private courts. And doubtless he concluded that Sabbath's kind of 'stupidity' had its rewards as he strode the corridors of his mansion, viewing the lines of gold and platinum albums on the walls of the billiards room, that celebrated some fourteen million sales, or the fine art paintings that decorated the rest of the house, one of them a portrait in oils of Susan. If he felt mournful at such attacks he could accompany his mood at the harp or harmonium that graced one of the state rooms.

Oh the folly of it all. Asked if he enjoyed being rich and famous Tony responded swiftly; 'I want to move – to a bigger house!' And yet Tony Iommi is not noted for being one of rock's more extrovert characters off stage. He admitted as much when he talked to Keith Altham in the NME in the early Seventies. 'I'm basically a shy person and don't like meeting people. I prefer to stay home, watching TV and playing monopoly.'

Some might feel this was a boring existence but

Tony said the explanation was simple. 'I've done my raving. If I do go out to a club now it's just the same old stupid questions. "When are you playing again" and "what is the new album called?" I get so cheesed off with it. I stopped going out. We were living too fast on the road as it was.'

Away from the din of Sabbath, Iommi, the creator of rock's heaviest band found peace and comfort in the music of Peter, Paul and Mary, Frank Sinatra, the Moody Blues and the Carpenters, whose albums he played while sipping a refreshing cup of tea, and browsing through a copy of **Country Life**.

Such contentment seemed to elude Ozzy however. He had the joy and comfort of his own family but by September 1976 he announced that he was leaving them to go to America, ostensibly to escape the clutches of the taxman. He planned to leave Britain in the spring of 1977 to become a tax exile leaving behind his wife Thelma and their three children, Jessica, Louis and Eliot, at their home in Ranton, Staffs.

Said Ozzy: 'I cannot go on paying 83p in the pound to the tax man and if I'm to provide for the future of my family, I must leave Britain by the beginning of the next financial year. At the moment America is my first choice. It will break my heart to leave the family but trailing around after a rock band is no life for small children.'

Thelma told the Sunday Mirror: 'It might sound odd for a family who love each other to live in different countries but we honestly think this is the best solution.' Ozzy assured the family he would be able to come back and visit them.* All this presaged another, equally dramatic split. It wasn't long before the rumours began to circulate that Sabbath was about to break up. The truth was that Ozzy yearned to break free and plunge into his own solo career. When you are entrenched in a popular, successful band earning lots of money, it required nerves of steel, or at least Ozzy's 'look before you leap' temperament to take the plunge. Sabbath and their manager officially denied the split rumours and it was announced that a new British tour would begin in the Autumn. In fact it was part of a world tour which included a mysterious 'fifth member' of the band, keyboard player Gerald Woodruffe, brought in to fill out their sound and help recreate the sound of such albums as *Sabotage*.

His presence was a well-kept secret for some time and indeed he was kept hidden in the wings — dressed in suitable stage gear but screened from the eyes of Sabbath fans who might have considered him an intruder. Certainly his contribution gave more freedom for Tony on guitar. But why was poor Gerald kept hidden? 'Because he's ugly,' shortled Ozzy. When he could be prevailed upon to cease shortling he allowed: 'He's not a member of the group — he's a technician.'

Sabbath could be rather tough on fellow musicians. Tony was aloof on the road and kept to his own dressing room, while support bands were kept in their place. Girlschool supported Sabbath on a 1980 tour and felt somewhat slighted by their new singer Ronnie James Dio. They had no time for sound checks and what rankled most was when Bill Ward sent a roadie over to ask one of them for a cigarette. But then Sabbath were long in tooth and too road weary to be bothered with the sensitivities of young upstarts. It had been a hard road for them and perhaps they felt it would do newcomers some good to be put to the test.

But back in 1976, before the split, the band were still looking for a way to progress and update their sound resulting in the release in October of *Technical Ecstasy* which was distinguished, apart from the quality of the music, by the cover picture of two robots 'screwing on an escalator' as it was graphically

*On July 4, 1982 Ozzy remarried, to his manager Sharon Arden, Don's daughter, in a ceremony at Maui, Hawaii.

described by the singer with the band. The same year they released the compilation album *We Sold Our Soul For Rock'n'Roll* which included *Black Sabbath*, *Paranoid*, *Sabbath Bloody Sabbath*, *Snowblind* and *Am I Going Insane?* culled from previous albums. By this time the original *Paranoid* LP had sold a million copies.

Technical Ecstasy was hailed as a milestone in the group's career, but some thought it was just an example of the band losing their way. Says heavy metal expert Malcolm Dome of 'Metal Mania': 'Albums like *Never Say Die* and *Technical Ecstasy* weren't going anywhere. It was just Black Sabbath rushing around looking for something to hold onto apart from their past reputation.'

It may have been that this change of direction was a result of the continued desire by Tony Iommi to seek a musical excellence and status that other groups enjoyed, a movement that Ozzy didn't in his heart embrace with much enthusiasm.

In a candid moment (all Ozzy's moments are candid), he commented on *Technical Ecstasy* in wry tones: 'It's a good album, it was enjoyable to make – well Tony enjoyed it. He made it.' He agreed that the band had undergone changes. 'We used to write songs about how lousy the world is and it was right for the time. But now we know that everyone realises the world is bad so we've changed our approach.'

'We're telling people stories in our music these days. I only hope they enjoy them.' The old brotherly togetherness of the band was beginning to show signs of cracking. Said Ozzy: 'For one thing, we don't see each other as much as we did before. We speak on the 'phone more than meet and when we meet it's rehearsals or being on the road. But that's okay because we've all got things to do individually and when we get together we're the mates we've always been. It's rare for a band to stay together as long as we have and that just doesn't happen by accident. We've changed as people but I think we've matured a lot as well. You can't stay in the music business for years and not mature. You either grow up and care about what you're doing or else you pack in. We're not going to stop because what we do is too important to us and I like to think that there's a lot of kids who think it's important too. Everybody knows the world is crap but there's good things in it and maybe for some people we're one of them.'

For Tony Iommi *Technical Ecstasy* represented the album that put all thoughts of their management hassles behind them. He could stop thinking about lawyers and concentrate on music. Said Bill Ward: 'Tony followed it all the way through from the first scratch, sitting in a room and writing the songs, to the last scratch, in the mastering and cutting rooms.' Said Tony: 'This album is our best ever. The whole band is better than ever. Most of the songs on *Technical Ecstasy* are stage songs so we'll be performing most of them on tour. They're songs I feel good about because they're all ours, in every sense of the phrase. We're a playing band and we need to be on stage and play to people. It's what Sabbath has always done and it's something we always will do, if we can.

'Our new songs are different. They're a different direction for us. Instead of being out and out heavy the songs are being tackled in a different way.' Tony explained that the heavy material of the past expressed how they felt at the time of their creation. But they had to progress to stay alive. The rest of the band supported Tony to the hilt in his changes, and enthused Bill Ward: 'Tony is amazing. With the new songs he's written he's surprised me more than ever. The dedication he puts into Sabbath is incredible. His guitar playing is better than ever and some of his new licks just amaze me.'

Geezer Butler during that 1977 tour also took time out to review Sabbath's development. He thought the tour was probably the most important they had done in terms of keeping the band established in the public's mind. 'We could never be a studio band. That's not the way we do things,' he said. 'But we're not too bad in the studio either, because this latest album is one of the best for a long time. There's a better feeling on the whole album than anything we've done before. We've changed a lot. We're all older and we're all alcoholics. And we've slowed down a lot. That's what happens when you've got one foot in the grave. From a personal point of view we see things in a bit more perspective. It's all less black and white than it used to be. The lyrics have been influenced by that. Musically we've become a helluva lot more mature although we still play heavy stuff. There's a lot more things coming out – like Bill singing one of the songs on the album which you wouldn't believe.' Geezer saw this as an example of how the band were ready to try new things. He may not have suspected that it was an unconscious nudge at Ozzy's position.

Geezer just hoped that Sabbath would win more respect from the rock community by its attempts at progression and told reporters 'I hope we've got through all that heat about being a loud band and all that. Of course we're loud but the point is we use amplification in a reasonable way. I remember how people always used to argue about who was the loudest band in the world. It was us or Deep Purple. But it doesn't mean anything. I don't care what other bands are doing. I'm just interested in what I'm doing. And I like music loud – but good loud.'

For his part, Ozzy had long ago forcibly expressed his beliefs in what rock and Sabbath were all about, and musical progression was not something he pursued with relish. In a 1972 interview with NME's Tony Stewart he said: 'I go out on stage and I think, "Fuck it man, all we are anyway is a rock'n'roll band." I just can't stand to see a band on stage trying to baffle the audience. I've been to the Marquee and seen groups and they're just playing bollocks man, complete and utter rubbish.'

'And the kids . . . you can see them looking and thinking, "Wow man, I don't dig this, but it must be good." They go "Hip, hip, hooray, Peace." And all this shit. When I go on stage I want to get people to dance. I don't want people to think this is an A minor, or D, F sharp . . . they're only ordinary people in an ordinary club.'

One wonders what band it was that caused Ozzy's hackles to rise — King Crimson, or the Mahavishnu Orchestra perhaps? He postulated the theory that Sabbath played 'basic music for basic people' and of progressive rock he stated quite categorically 'I don't dig it at all. It just never turned me on. I must be a nut case but I just get pissed off and bored with it all. I dig Humble Pie. If you can stamp your feet to it and nod your head, it's good as far as I'm concerned. It's good old rock'n'roll and God bless it man because that's what it's all about for me.'

On March 12 1977 the band started their UK tour at the Glasgow Apollo, greeted with hysteria as green spotlights glowed through the fog of dry ice and fans gave the eternal peace signs. It was an emotional night for Glasgow. But later that year, in November 1977, Ozzy stunned Sabbath fans by announcing his departure from the group. Tony, Geezer and Bill decided that however big a following Ozzy had, they could not just throw away the whole concept of the band and simply retire. And in any case they were probably tired of his unpredictable behaviour. At first it was suggested Deep Purple singer David Coverdale might replace him. Instead they brought in a Birmingham lad, Dave Walker who had been in local bands like the Red Caps, Idle Race, Savoy Brown and American band Mistress. But he only made one appearance as lead singer with Sabbath, on a BBC Midlands TV show. Ozzy came back in January 1978, just in time for the band's tenth anniversary world tour, and *Never Say Die* album.

Said Ozzy: 'I tried working with other guys but these days bands haven't got it together as much as they used to have. The first thing they want to talk about is money which is really the last thing that concerns me. My view is that if you've got enough bread to scrape by on, then you're alright. I missed the family atmosphere of Black Sabbath. I had a rest, but knew in my heart that I was making a mistake and I just had to get back in there.'

The band played at Madison Square in September and 20,000 kids screamed in response to a reunited Sabbath. But their days with Ozzy were numbered. Meanwhile fans lit candles and held wooden crosses. A touching spectacle if somewhat baffling to students of human relationships. What did it all mean? Ozzy could only explain it in terms of the interaction between performers and audience.

Staggering off stage after a Madison Square concert Ozzy said: 'Just listen to them . . . they were fantastic. I'm a wreck but that reaction makes it all worth while. I come alive only when I'm on stage.' He told Ken Irwin of the Daily Mirror: 'It takes me hours to wind down afterwards. We played Madison Square before, it's always like climbing Mount Everest.'

The week of September 4, 1978 as the band celebrated their tenth anniversary they also enjoyed the spectacle of the single *Never Say Die* from the album of the same name, hitting 21 in the UK charts. The world tour took the band through some thirty concerts before Christmas with the prospect of a tour of Japan and Australia in the following year. The strain was beginning to tell.

Said Ozzy: 'All the travelling is an absolute killer. We used to fly everywhere in the States so we saw nothing but the inside of aeroplanes and hotels. After a few months touring we would all stagger back home thin as rakes because we were not eating properly. And we all had nervous breakdowns. Now we have our own specially equipped bus. We sleep on it and see much more of the countryside.'

Once again Ozzy looked back with some amazement at his personal career and tried to relate to the wild and irresponsible youth who had set out in Birmingham back in the dark ages.

'As a kid I was a ruffian — a real tearaway. I tried all kinds of jobs but ended up as a professional burglar. One day I got caught breaking into a house and was sent to prison. It was a real lesson to me. After that I got together with the other lads to form a band. Music saved me from becoming a hardened criminal.'

Ozzy revealed that one of the reasons he had left the band for a while was because his father had been dying. 'I was heartbroken when my father died but at least he saw that I had made something of a success of my life before he went. That meant a lot to me.'

How had Black Sabbath managed to stick together for ten years? 'It must be super glue,' said Ozzy. Just weeks after that cheery riposte the glue began to lose its adhesive properties. On November 11, 1978 newspaper headlines described a 'Police kidnap alert' when Ozzy failed to turn up for a sell-out concert in Nashville, Tennessee. Some 12,000 fans were told the night's concert was cancelled. Albert Chapman was convinced Ozzy must have been kidnapped. It just wasn't Ozzy's style to miss a gig. But it turned out the exhausted singer had been fast asleep in his hotel bed. The wrong hotel bed.

Said Albert: 'I searched every bar in town even though I knew Ozzy never drank before a performance.' Then came the explanations. Ozzy had stumbled back to the hotel for sleep and had gone into somebody else's bedroom by mistake. To make up for the missed show, the group put on an extra performance.

But it wasn't long before the final curtain fell on Ozzy's relationship with Black Sabbath and he quit the band the following year. At least they had survived ten years together through hell and high volume. Now a new decade and astonishing developments loomed.

CHAPTER 9
OZZY, BLOODY OZZY

Great groups are those which develop a bond of unswerving loyalty with their followers by reason of a whole variety of virtues and vices. The bands which struggle, which wear their hearts on their sleeve and can be seen to be adhering to whatever principles first motivated them, are those who can lay claim to glory built on the most solid foundations.

Groups in this category which spring to mind are Genesis, the Who, Yes and Black Sabbath. And in all cases, when a member chooses to leave the group and they are affected by some drastic shake-up, then fans' loyalty is put to the test. People resent change and can be hostile to new faces who are often seen as usurpers. But in most cases, when the dust has settled, if the right choices and changes have been made, then quarrels are patched up and transgressions forgiven, except perhaps by a minority of die-hards. The same has long been true of the world of jazz. Rock fans would be astonished to know that jazz enthusiasts are still mourning the departure of trumpeter Cootie Williams from the Duke Ellington Orchestra of 1940 and the premature end of the partnership between Dizzy Gillespie and Charlie Parker.

Yes fans were plunged into despair by the endless changes in line-up during the Seventies and Genesis afficionados were shaken to the core by the departure of Peter Gabriel. It seemed nothing would ever be the same again, and doom was predicted for both singer and group. As we now know, history proved otherwise.

It was a blow when Ozzy Osbourne quit Black Sabbath in 1979 and few observers gave either parties much chance of survival. Sabbath without Ozzy was like a bat with its head cut off. Geezer, Tony and Bill had done their jobs well but Ozzy gave Sabbath its visual focus and communication with the people.

Likewise Ozzy was too much of a maverick to make a success of his own band. Cancelled gigs and muddles over personnel seemed to confirm this jaundiced view. He had sheltered too long behind the Sabbath organisation. But on both counts the doubters were hopelessly wrong. Sabbath did not give up the ghost and die. It rattled past the graveyards of rock in a chariot of fiery determination. And Ozzy launched a veritable blizzard of publicity about his activities which combined with strong musical output resulted in an astonishing conquest of America that left him breathless, and almost speechless.

First reports of Ozzy's departure said that while Sabbath were in Los Angeles preparing for an American tour in September, Ozzy had been sent back to England by the rest of the band under orders to 'get himself together' before the tour. Ronnie Dio was rehearsing with the remaining members of the group but the management then stressed that he would not be taking over from Ozzy on a permanent basis. Dio was just 'helping out and would not be touring with the group.' They added that Ozzy has left the band several times before and had always come back. Indeed Ozzy was not alone in this practice of taking the odd Sabbatical.

In July 1979 Geezer walked out on the band in California and was replaced by Geoff Nicols (ex-Quartz guitarist and keyboard player who was also produced by Tony Iommi). Eventually Ronnie was made the permanent replacement for Ozzy and Geezer went off the boil and returned to the fold in 1980 for the *Heaven And Hell* album and 1980 British tour. It was also the year Bill Ward quit the band.

Ronnie James Dio had been tearing his throat out with Ritchie Blackmore's Rainbow. Ronnie, from New York City, used to sing with a band called Elf under his real name of Ronald Padavona. He was discovered by Deep Purple's Roger Glover and Ian Paice during a 1972 American tour and they were immediately impressed by his singing style. They offered to produce Elf's first album which appeared on Epic. Elf later supported Purple on their American tours which brought Ronnie to the attention of Ritchie Blackmore. They also came to Britain with Purple in 1974. After months of rumour and speculation Ritchie decided to quit the super successful Purple in April 1975 and planned his own band, to be called Rainbow. His lead singer was Ronnie Dio and the combination, with Cozy Powell on drums led to the creation of a classic group. But Rainbow were smitten with more line-up changes than John Mayall's Bluesbreakers (well, almost), and Ronnie left in January 1979.

The revitalised Sabbath released the *Heaven And Hell* album in April 1980 with all the lyrics credited to Ronnie and music written and arranged by the rest of the band. The result was a fast moving and confident sound that reflected the re-birth of the heavy metal movement.

It seemed a promising new start to the band's career but their elation was tempered by events in America. During their US tour in October 1980 the 7,000 strong audience at Milwaukee turned nasty and began hurling bottles, one of which hit Geezer Butler who had to be taken to hospital suffering from facial cuts. Dozens were injured in fighting including eight cops.

Geezer was hit in the face as soon as the band began playing and the band immediately started to pack up. Staff man Ian Ferguson was also hit by a bottle as he attempted to move the equipment. Then 150 police stormed into the arena while the mob threw chairs, fireworks and bottles, smashed phones, broke windows and fought each other. Geezer needed three stitches. The power of the peace sign seemed to have evaporated.

More trouble followed the band to Britain and there was a riot by a thousand fans at the Sophia Gardens Pavilion, Cardiff in January 1981 when six fans were arrested. But this time there was some excuse for the violence as many fans had tickets but could not get into the concert. The situation was calmed when the band promised to play another hour and a half show.

After a long and honourable career, Bill Ward left the band in November 1980 during the American tour to be replaced by the dynamic Vinnie Appice, hailed as one of the loudest drummers – even without a PA – in the world. Vinnie was brother of Carmine, who had formed a mutual admiration society with John Bonham in the days of Vanilla Fudge and Led Zeppelin. So there were family ties between Birmingham and California. It was this new Anglo-American Sabbath which produced *Mob Rules*, with a startling LP cover by Greg Hildebrant, which helped confirm Sabbath's position at the forefront of heavy rock in 1981.

Said Ronnie about Bill's departure: 'He had already left the band a couple of times and we sympathised as he had suffered some very heavy personal losses.' (His mother and father had died quite close together). 'We managed to pull him back in. But eventually it became too much for us and for him. He couldn't cope with being on the road anymore. In the end we decided to part company on the best of terms. Everybody in the group still loves the man dearly and wishes him all the best.'

Bill carried on playing and joined a local band in Los Angeles where he settled down to live, US Government officials permitting.

At the beginning of 1982 Sabbath were at last receiving the critical praise which had so often eluded them in the past. When in December they played sell-out shows at London's Odeon Hammersmith, critics including MM's Brian Harrigan spoke of 'their new vitality and infinitely improved stage show.' This featured a remarkable stage set by LSD, the Birmingham based Light & Sound Design, which depicted a church yard, with the drum riser got up to look like a tombstone.

Tour dates were Odeon Hammersmith December 31, 1981 and January 1, 2, 3, Newcastle City Hall (5/6), Royal Highland Hall, Edinburgh (8), Bingley Hall, Stafford (9), Queen's Hall, Leeds (12) and St. Austell Coliseum, Cornwall (14). By now tickets were £5 a concert compared to the 18s. of ten years earlier.

The band were incredibly loud – so nothing had changed in that department. And on one night when the PA packed up, both Ronnie's vocals and Vinnie's drums carried to the back of the hall without any need for amplification. Said one ear-witness. 'It was so bloody loud, I couldn't stand it. I had to go.' But the majority of Sabbath fans were overjoyed at the band's return and greeted them with blazing cigarette lighters, wooden crucifixes, a flurry of long hair and loon pants and the wafting aroma of patchouli oil that scents all able-bodied metal freaks.

The band spent most of the previous few months in America touring and had missed an English gig when they pulled out of the Heavy Metal Holocaust held in Stoke on Trent in August 1981. Ironically the band were replaced by Ozzy Osbourne. Sabbath explained that during that period they had been involved in recording *Mob Rules* which was released in October. The work on the album was done at The Record Plant in L.A. and was delayed a couple of months which meant they couldn't come to England for the 'Holocaust.' The fact that Ozzy was booked by the irate promoter to fill in for them didn't help already soured relations between the old partners. Geezer Butler told Brian Harrigan: 'I haven't seen Ozzy in ages. And as far as animosity between us goes it all seems to be on Ozzy's side. Everytime he does an interview he spends more time talking about us than about himself. Obviously we're feeling a bit bitter about what he's saying.'

And what Ozzy was saying was that Tony and Geezer were ruining the name of Black Sabbath. He had been hurt and annoyed when he realised they would carry on using the name after he left. Said Geezer: 'He keeps on about how we shouldn't have kept the name after he left. He reckons he wrote all the songs, he thinks he thought of the name originally. And lately he's been saying we had to pay him off to leave the band. All that is totally ridiculous. It's a shame he has taken this kind of attitude because he's successful in his own right now.'

Geezer described Sabbath's trials and troubles during the change-over period. 'It's not been easy over the last year or so. On this last tour we had to prove ourselves all over again. People don't accept a band until they've heard them and seen them and I suppose with Ronnie as lead singer and now Vinnie Appice as drummer we're a different band to the Sabbath that everyone's known over the years.

'So people had to know that we could do it. That doesn't just mean the public either. That includes the record company who aren't going to get behind you until you've proved you can do it. Obviously we did because on this tour we're getting a lot of support and co-operation. I feel as though we've made it all over again.'

Some critics thought that Sabbath were still living on past glories – playing the old tunes like *Paranoid* and *Iron Man*. But the group had tried pulling them out of their repertoire many times in the past and they always had to put them back in again due to pressure of public demand. The fans felt cheated if they didn't hear their favourite Sabbath songs. And they let the group know; in letters and in person during and after the concerts. Sabbath audiences can always be relied on to speak their minds.

What difference had the arrival of Ronnie Dio made? Said Geezer: 'There was nothing new coming out of the numbers Ozzy was doing in the last days of the band with him. But when Ronnie came in he really made a hell of a difference. He writes lyrics, which takes a lot of that pressure off me and he's not afraid to speak his mind. If he thinks something's crap he'll tell you and that's the best way to be.'

Geezer enthused about the arrival of Vinnie Appice, ex-Rick Derringer. 'He's a great drummer and he had fitted in perfectly. He didn't have much chance to ease himself in. We were in the States and Bill got some bad news from home (his father died), and so he just left. He said he was going and he went

immediately. You can't blame the bloke and he's still one of the Sabbath family, don't make any mistake about that.'

The group missed their old pal who had so often been the victim of practical jokes in the past – like the night Ozzy decided he wanted to rip Bill's shirt off to enliven a dull stay in a London hotel, and it ended up with them tearing each other's clothes off.

When Bill left, his departure caused an immediate problem. They had to cancel a concert in Denver at a 20,000 seater stadium which enraged the local promoter.

Vinnie came into the band at two days notice and soon got to grips with Sabbath music. 'Ronnie and Vinnie have given me and Tony a kick up the arse,' Geezer said. 'They've really geed us up and I honestly think we're enjoying it more now than we've ever done. I reckon we're playing better than we have for years.'

Also bringing comfort and security to the band was the knowledge that their affairs are now sympathetically handled by American Sandy Pearlman, a rock critic turned manager. Said Geezer: 'We're making sure we keep well up with the business side of things. We're taking more control of that side than ever before. We've had a few problems in the past and with Sandy Pearlman we're working together to make sure that kind of thing doesn't happen again.'

Sabbath recorded many of the gigs on their end

of '81 tour partly to counteract the release of the *Live At Last* album which had aroused some anger within the group. Geezer described it as 'that bloody awful album.' He explained: 'It went out last year without our approval and we didn't like it. Problem was it sold well and we reckoned that was simply because a lot of kids wanted to hear a live Sabbath album. So we've decided to do one ourselves, and do it properly.'

Sabbath promise they will go on working in the years to come making more albums and continuing their annual round of tours, just as they have done these past 14 years.

Said Geezer: 'There was a time when I thought I'd had enough of all that, but these days I'm enjoying it more and more. We're probably going to go on forever. That should upset a lot of people.'

Ozzy, unpredictable, outrageous and loveable confounded all who prophesied doom in the wake of his departure from Sabbath. Within a year of launching his solo career with the Blizzard Of Ozz band he achieved platinum album sales and a worldwide following. The star was re-born, and despite his soured relationship with the old band, there was no stopping Ozzy, Bloody Ozzy. The new band signed to Don Arden's Jet Records. Comprising American musicians Randy Rhoads (guitar), Rudy Sarzo (bass) and Tommy Aldridge (drums), they were a tough line-up well equipped to compete with the best bands on the Eighties' scene.

Ozzy had been in despair of finding the right musicians when he finally met Randy Rhoads who had been in a Log Angeles band called Quiet Riot. He was teaching music at a local college when Ozzy tracked him down. The first formation of the Blizzard actually included bassist Bob Daisley (ex-Rainbow, and a colleague of Ronnie Dio who replaced Ozzy in Sabbath), and Lee Kerslake, ex-Uriah Heep on drums. Both Kerslake and Daisley left in May 1981 to be replaced by Tommy Aldridge, formerly the drummer with Black Oak Arkansas and Pat Travers, and bassist Rudy Sarzo, who had also been in Quiet Riot. This band made its debut tour of America in May 1981.

Ozzy called his new music simply 'Ozzy Music' and refused to accept the 'heavy metal' tag but it was certainly his personality which helped them gain world wide success, compounded by the release of the *Diary Of A Madman* album in October 1981, a project he had conceived years before. Indeed ex-Sabbath publicist Keith Goodwin recalls seeing Ozzy wearing a 'Blizzard Of Ozz' tee-shirt way back in the early Seventies, which shows how long ideas had been fermenting.

It seemed that everything was perfectly wizard for the Great Oz during 1981 and he said as much. 'I'd been trying to get my own band together long before I'd officially left Sabbath. The first real attempt I made was in Los Angeles. I was over there working in a studio with Gary Moore and Glenn Hughes also got involved.

'Glenn didn't last very long with us,' said Ozzy, 'but Gary was really involved. Gary is such a phenomenal player. He's really genuinely brilliant. He would have been great to work with but he wanted to get his own band together, and I wanted to get mine.' (Gary went on to form the short lived G-Force and then worked with Greg Lake's band).

'I don't think our ideas were really the same and I think both of us really wanted to be the boss of the band and there wouldn't have been room for the two of us. To be honest I think Gary was a bit too good for me. My whole idea was to get back to basics in any band that I was getting together. I needed really hard driving, really heavy music, straightforward stuff that kids could really get into.'

This was the nub of the matter – the reason for the break with Sabbath. The rest of the band didn't see eye to eye with him on basic rock principles. And Ozzy had no doubt that Tony Iommi was his main adversary in this department. When they were kids, starting out, Ozzy took it all in his stride, but with age attitudes harden and tolerance levels diminish. This nagging difference in attitudes had grown to unmanagable proportions.

Said Ozzy: 'I wasn't really happy with Black Sabbath and the way things were going over the last two or three albums before I left. I mean, it was really getting away from everything that Sabbath had been based on in the first place. What we needed was a good strong producer who could direct us in the studio and someone who wasn't too directly involved in the band personally. Instead we were trying to produce ourselves and we were getting lost.' For once Ozzy shared the same opinion as some critics.

'Tony was always trying to make the band more sophisticated. I mean there was one time when he brought in a whole load of string players on a session. I walked into the studio and there were all these guys of about 50 sitting around waiting for their go. I thought to myself "What the hell is all this?" I mean – violinists on a Black Sabbath album! If I'd been a fan I wouldn't have believed it. As a matter of fact I WAS a fan and I didn't believe it.

'I didn't think that any Black Sabbath fans wanted to listen to that kind of stuff. It just wasn't us. On stage Tony used to go into these great long guitar solos which were like jazz. I mean – jazz at a Black Sabbath gig – ridiculous. I used to watch him from the side of the stage and cringe when Tony did that sort of thing. I used to hide. I'm not knocking him technically because I still think he's a really brilliant guitar player. But his jazz solos used to slow things down so much.'

'Anyway we came to a crossroads in the band. I was uncomfortable and I couldn't really decide whether to go or to stay. Whatever I suggested the band didn't like. No one listened to me at all and that's a real drag. You've got no idea how that feels. You can't keep on going in a situation like that.

'Anyway, we decided to pack it in – the whole band. We were going to do a farewell tour and that would be the end of it. The band would split up and the name wouldn't be used by any members. But it didn't work out like that. The farewell tour never happened and the band met up with Ronnie before I went to Los Angeles to see about my band. They just got him in and carried on as Sabbath.

'I'm not bitter about that but honestly I was surprised the way things turned out because I thought everything had been decided as far as farewell tours and all that were concerned. I was a bit surprised really.'

Ozzy and his band jumped in to play at the Heavy Metal Holocaust at Stoke when Sabbath dropped out. He took a couple of days off from an American tour to fly over for the festival. He had to return the following morning and Ozzy was most upset that he was able to spend only a few hours with his wife Thelma and their children. He was exhausted by the show and despairing of the crisis in his life. He told writer James Johnson that his wife had once persuaded him to take psychiatric treatment, and he spent several months recovering from the ravages of rock.

'I didn't know which end of the day it was,' he said. 'I was taking drugs so much I was a wreck. The final straw was when I shot all our cats. We had about seventeen and I went crazy and shot them all. My wife found me under the piano in a white suit holding a shot gun in one hand a knife in the other.'

Ozzy's reputation for ill-treating animals had become to grow and caused a devastating reaction in America. At home too the music press readers' columns were bombarded with letters of complaint. Ozzy once made the grim but cruelly humourous aside in an interview: 'I used to work with horses. I used to strangle them.' Then he went for broke and at an American record company reception, he bit the head off a dove. To complete the evolution of his role as a modern day Count Dracula, he bit the head of a bat. People were understandably shocked and outraged by these exploits. Had the madman gone too far? In America the backlash resembled the kind of reaction John Lennon sparked when he said the Beatles were more popular than Jesus Christ.

Some could see it all as a joke and begged newspapers to re-print the picture of the dove incident. It occured when Ozzy decided to enliven an American press reception thrown by his record company. He felt an instinctive dislike for record company bosses who he considered were more interested in enjoying their annual convention trips than anything Ozzy was doing. The original idea was to release a couple of doves, symbols of peace, at the party. To the horror of everyone present, Ozzy succumbed to one of his 'compulsive moments' that had been his characteristic since his days as a 13-year-old semi-professional burglar. He bit the head off one of the doves and instantly achieved notoriety throughout America. The bat affair followed not long after at a Des Moines concert.

Ozzy's stage act had by now developed to the point where it made Alice Cooper's show look like Camel on a dull night. He employed a midget whose task it was to throw liver and other items of offal at the audience, and who was subsequently 'hanged' live on stage. American kids, following the tradition of the movie 'Carrie' responded by bringing the blood soaked remains of slaughtered animals to the shows to throw back. One group of teenagers was arrested trying to smuggle a cow's head into one auditorium. Someone who had got past the police guard tossed a bat on stage and Ozzy being Ozzy, he immediately grabbed it and stuffed it in his mouth in an attempt at repeating his dove beheading routine. The bat was alive, retaliated and bit Ozzy back. Fearful of catching rabies, Ozzy was rushed to hospital for injections. The fate of the partially chewed bat is unknown but Ozzy later collapsed on stage in Illinois, due to the delayed effects of his injections. The bat had its revenge.

The band's keyboard player Don Airey, who had joined them just after Christmas, told what happened. 'Somebody threw a bat on stage. Ozzy thought it was a plastic one so he put it in his mouth, without thinking. When he told me afterwards that he'd put a dead bat in his mouth I said "You're joking!" But in the end we took him to hospital and he went in barking. When the nurse asked him what he'd got he just barked and told her it was rabies. She didn't believe him and asked again. Then a look of horror came over her face. We had a police escort to another hospital where the serum is kept. Ozzy went in barking but came out a sadder and wiser man. Now he's got to have injections every four days.'

'He's still going around barking so we just do our best to keep out of his way.'

An early stint working in a slaughterhouse may well have numbed Ozzy's natural human sensitivity when it came to animal welfare. He could look any critic in the eye and accuse them of hypocrisy when he knew what he knew about the way the Western world is fed. He cited the case of Col. Sanders and his chickens. Many more of these had been dispatched than Ozzy had rubbed out doves or bats. And as a hunter who strode around his country estate armed with a gun, he claimed he shot for food, not for fun.

As the tour continued and the headlines mounted, Ozzy seemed determined, as the radio commercials ran, 'to turn the United States into a mental state.'

He was taking great risks, but as he told MM's Allan Jones in a revealing interview: 'It is getting heavy. Anything sensational they just go for it. I'm desperately frightened that some guy's going to blow me away. Some of these guys are nuts. They want to take it too far. All it is you know, I'm a clown. A terrible old showbiz ham. I'm not a musician. I'm not a singer. So why do they take it all so seriously? I just get people off. I'm their joint if you like. They smoke me and they get high.' Ozzy insisted that if people thought he was having a bad effect on the minds of young kids, they should go and watch the TV news where real murder and mayhem were a way of life, and shown night after night.

Ozzy stepped up his frontal assault on American sensibilities when he peed in front of the nation's most sacred shrine, the Alamo. He had gone their for a picture session, and suddenly caught short, decided to drop his trousers and relieve himself in front of the old fort, scene of the famed battle for Texan independence. He was reported to the police, arrested and spent a night in a cell in San Antonio, sharing the facilities, he said, with a murderer. It reminded him of his incarceration in Winson Green. Unrepentant he claimed that his new goal in life was to 'piss on the steps of the Whitehouse.'

It reached the point where Ozzy was accused of being 'the anti-Christ' and ministers of religion pleaded with fans not to go inside his concerts.

Worse was to come. Much worse. For in the midst of all the showbiz shennanigans and leg pulling, suddenly real tragedy struck. Maybe the build up of hysteria and madness surrounding the tour, communicated to others associated with Ozzy. At any rate, on the morning of March 19, 1982 a pilot took up the band's guitarist Randy Rhoads for a trip in a light plane. They began mock diving bombing runs over the truck containing the rest of the band. Suddenly one wing clipped the truck and the plane crashed into the ground, killing those on board including Randy. It was a devastating blow to everybody and Ozzy was distraught, numbed by the tragic waste and the loss of his friend. He had to think long and hard and decided the only course was to carry on touring, if only to prevent his own personal breakdown. There should be no time for brooding. Work was the only solace and a fitting tribute to Randy. Guitarist Bernie Torme was rushed out to replace Randy and the band staggered on. Only a few days before Ozzy had been contemplating the dreadful mortality rate in rock. 'I suppose the same thing's going to happen to me one day. The price you pay I suppose. The death rate in rock'n'roll is phenomenal. You live at 100 miles per hour, 24 hours a day. And your body can only take so much stress.'

The lighter flames glowed for Randy, and Ozzy and Black Sabbath, and the crucifixes were raised as the hysteria and confusion that has surrounded them from the earliest times reached a crescendo. One day the flames will dim. But Ozzy, Sabbath and their fans can look back on one hell fire of a career.

CHAPTER 10
BORN AGAIN

Black Sabbath and Ozzy Osbourne's careers underwent drastic changes in the years after their traumatic split. Ozzy has enjoyed remarkable success in America but seems cursed with bad luck. The heaviest blow was the death of his friend and guitarist Randy Rhoads. Then came some more cheering news when he married his manager Sharon Arden, Don's daughter. In a ceremony at Maui, Hawaii on July 4, 1982 the couple were pictured with Sharon in white and Ozzy in Dracula fangs. His mother and sister were among the guests who sampled wedding cake laced with two bottles of brandy.

Ozzy remained at loggerheads with his old group, and recorded a double 'live' album *Talk Of The Devil* (Jet DP 401) on which he performed all of Sabbath's best known songs. His band featured Brad Gillis (guitar), Rudi Sarzo (bass) and Tommy Aldridge (drums) and they recreated hits like *Symptom Of The Universe*, *War Pigs* and even *Fairies Wear Boots* and *Black Sabbath*.

It must have rubbed salt into the wounds of the split but later there came an emotional reunion. Said Geezer Butler 'Ozzy slagged us to death after he left us, but when we saw him after two years, he came to our hotel at four in the morning and we had a really great time. All the bad feeling was forgotten. We were genuinely pleased when Ozzy happened in America'.

After the death of Rhoads, Ozzy went through a succession of guitarists including Bernie Torme, Brad Gillis and Pete Way. Said Ozzy 'Sometimes I woke up in the morning and wondered who was still in the band.' Eventually he settled on American axe man Jake E. Lee.

Ozzy became a notorious figure in America and there were even death threats from religious fanatics who took stories of his gothic horror stage act too seriously. He quit Jet Records and signed to Epic and released his first album for them, called *Bark At The Moon* in December 1983.

He had a new band with Bob Daisley (bass), Carmine Appice (drums), Jake E. Lee (guitar) and Don Airey (synthesiser), and embarked on a tour of Britain, America, Japan and Australia to take him into 1984.

Black Sabbath also experienced drastic upheavals when they parted company with their American lead singer Ronnie James Dio and drummer Vinnie Appice (Carmine's brother). Much to the surprise of fans, Ronnie was replaced by Ian Gillan, the Midlands born singer and high note specialist who had come to fame with Deep Purple and later found his own successful band, Gillan. When he broke up his own group there was a great row with accusations of treachery, particularly from Ian's bass player John McCoy. There was also much acrimony from Ronnie Dio.

But in February 1983 Gillan became the official lead singer with Black Sabbath. Their original drummer Bill Ward, was invited back into the fold. Unfortunately Bill had been suffering the effects of too much drinking over the years and could not make the band's summer tour. He was replaced by reliable ELO stalwart Bev Bevan and the new line up made its debut at the 1983 Reading Festival, where they got a mixed response from the crowd and critics.

Gillan proclaimed that he enjoyed being with Sabbath however and the team promptly went on to a tour of Europe visiting Spain, France and Germany. Said Ian: 'The thing is we've all come through the same clubs and pubs, we have the same sense of humour. It's gonna be a great crack. I'm looking forward to productive and exciting years ahead.'

Black Sabbath released a 'life' double album *Live Evil* in January 1983 and followed up with a new studio album with Ian Gillan, *Born Again* to rave reviews in August. With Bev Bevan as temporary drummer they took off for a tour of North America in the autumn of 1983.

Stop press: Feb 1984 – following a US tour Gillan leaves Sabbath. The story continues . . .

DISCOGRAPHY

SINGLE

Date	Title	Catalogue No.
January 1970	Evil Woman/Wicked World	Fontana TF 1067 – deleted
March 1970	Reissue – Evil Woman/Wicked World	Vertigo V2 – deleted
July 24 1970	Paranoid/The Wizard	Vertigo 6059 010 – deleted
September 1972	Tomorrow's Dream/Laguna Sunrise	Vertigo 6059 061 – deleted
December 1973	Sabbath Bloody Sabbath/Changes	WWA WWS 002 – deleted
February 1976	Am I Going Insane?/Hole In The Sky	NEMS 6165 300 – deleted
1977	Reissue – Paranoid/Snowblind	NEMS NES 112 – deleted
June 1978	Never Say Die/She's Gone	Vertigo SAB 1 – deleted
October 1978	Hard Road/Symptom Of The Universe	Vertigo SAB 2 – deleted
June 1980	Neon Knights/Children Of The Sea – live	Vertigo SAB 3 – deleted
June 1980	Reissue – Paranoid/Snowblind	NEMS BSS 101
November 1980	Die Young/Heaven And Hell	Vertigo SAB 4 – deleted
November 1980	Die Young/Heaven And Hell (12 inch)	Vertigo SAB 412
October 1981	Mob Rules/Die Young	Vertigo SAB 5 – deleted
October 1981	Mob Rules/Die Young (12 inch)	Vertigo SAB 512 – deleted
January 1982	Turn Up The Night/Lonely Is The Word (picture disc)	Vertigo SABP 6
January 1982	Turn Up The Night/Lonely Is The Word (12 inch picture disc)	Vertigo SABP 612
January 1982	Turn Up The Night/Lonely Is The Word (picture cover)	Vertigo SAB 6

OZZY OSBOURNE SINGLE

Date	Title	Catalogue No.
1981	Over The Mountain/I Don't Know (live)	Jet 7017
	Over The Mountain/I Don't Know (12 inch)	Jet 12017
December 1982	Symptom Of The Universe/N.I.B.	Jet 7030
	Symptom Of The Universe/Iron Man/Children Of The Grave (12 inch)	Jet 12030
November 1983	Bark At The Moon/Up The B Side	Epic A 3915
	Bark At The Moon/Up The B Side/Slow Down (12 inch version)	Epic TA 3915

ALBUMS

Date	Title/Tracks	Catalogue No.
February 13 1970	BLACK SABBATH – Black Sabbath; The Wizard; Behind The Wall Of Sleep; N.I.B.; Evil Woman; Sleeping Village; Warning	Vertigo VO 6 – deleted
Reissued in December 1973	BLACK SABBATH	WWA 006
Reissued in January 1976	BLACK SABBATH	NEMS NEL 6002 Also on Duth NEMS label
September 18 1970	PARANOID – War Pigs; Paranoid; Planet Caravan; Iron Man; Electric Funeral; Hand Of Doom; Rat Salad; Fairies Wear Boots	Vertigo 6360 011 – deleted
Reissued in December 1973	PARANOID	WWA 007
Reissued in January 1976	PARANOID	NEMS NEL 6003 WS 1887 Also on Italian Vertigo label and American Warner Brothers label
July 1971	MASTER OR REALITY – Sweet Leaf; After Forever; Embryo; Children Of The Grave; Orchid; Lord Of This World; Solitude; Into The Void	Vertigo 6360 050 – deleted

Date	Title/Tracks	Catalogue No.
Reissued in December 1973	MASTER OF REALITY	WWA 008
Reissued in February 1976	MASTER OF REALITY	NEMS NEL 6004 Also on Dutch NEMS label
September 1972	BLACK SABBATH VOLUME 4 – Wheels Of Confusion; Tomorrow's Dream; Changes; FX; Supernaut; Snowblind; Cornucopia; Laguna Sunrise; St. Vitus Dance; Under The Sun	Vertigo 6360 071 – deleted
Reissued in December 1973	BLACK SABBATH VOLUME 4	WWA 009
Reissued in February 1976	BLACK SABBATH VOLUME 4	NEMS NEL 6005

ALBUMS

Date	Title/Tracks	Catalogue Nol.
December 1973	SABBATH BLOODY SABBATH – Sabbath Bloody Sabbath; A National Acrobat; Fluff; Sabbra Cadabra; Killing Yourself To Live; Who Are You; Looking For Today; Spiral Architect	WWA 005 – deleted
Reissued in June 1980	SABBATH BLOODY SABBATH	NEMS NEL 6017 BS 2695 Also on Canadian Warner Brothers label
July 1975	SABOTAGE – Am I Going Insane?; Don't Start; Hole In The Sky; Megalomania; Supertzar; Symptom Of The Univers; Thrill Of It All; The Writ	NEMS 9199 001 – deleted
Reissued in June 1980	SABOTAGE	NEMS NEL 6018 BS 2822 Also on American Warner Brothers label
December 1975	WE SOLD OUR SOUL FOR ROCK'N'ROLL – (double album) – Am I Going Insane?; Black Sabbath; Changes; Children Of The Grave; Fairies Wear Boots; Iron Man; Laguna Sunrise; N.I.B.; Paranoid; Sabbath Bloody Sabbath; Snowblind; Sweet Leaf; Tomorrow's Dream; War Pigs; Warning; Wicked World; The Wizard	NEMS 6641 335 – deleted
Reissued in August 1976	WE SOLD OUR SOULD FOR ROCK'N'ROLL	NEMS NELD 101
October 1976	TECHNICAL ECSTASY – All Parts Moving; Bqck Street Kids; Dirty Women; Gypsy; It's Alright; Rock'n'Roll Doctor; She's Gone; You Won't Change Me	Vertigo 9102 750 – deleted
December 1977	GREATEST HITS – Paranoid; N.I.B.; Changes; Sabbath Bloody Sabbath; War Pigs; Laguna Sunrise; Tomorrow's Dream; Sweet Leaf	NEMS NEL 6009

ALBUMS

Date	Title/Tracks	Catalogue No.
October 1978	NEVER SAY DIE – Air Dance; Breakout; Hard Road; Johnn· Blade; Junior's Eyes; Never Say Die; Over To You; Shock Wave; Swinging The Chain	Vertigo 9102 751
April 1980	HEAVEN AND HELL – Children Of The Sea; Die Young; Heaven And Hell; Lady Evil; Lonely Is The Word; Neon Knights; Walk Away; Wishing Well	Vertigo 9102 752
June 1980	LIVE AT LAST – Tomorrow's Dream; Sweet Leaf; Killing Yourself To Live; Cornucopia; Snowblind; Children Of The Grave; War Pigs; Wicked World; Paranoid	NEMS BS 001
October 1981	MOB RULES – Turn Up The Night; Voodoo; The Sign Of The Southern Cross; E 5150; Mob Rules; Country Girl; Slippin' Away; Falling Off The Edge Of The World; Over And Over	Vertigo 6302 119
January 1983	LIVE EVIL – E5150; Neon Knights; N.I.B.; Children Of The Sea; Voodoo; Black Sabbath; War Pigs; Iron Man; Mob Rules; Heaven And Hell; The Sign Of The Southern Cross/Heaven And Hell Continued; Paranoid; Children Of The Grave; Fluff. (Features Vinnie Appice on drums and Ronnie James Dio vocals.)	Vertigo SAB 10
August 1983	BORN AGAIN – Trashed; Stonehenge; Disturbing The Priest; The Dark; Zero The Hero; Digital Bitch; Hot Line; Keep It Warm	Vertigo VERL 8

OZZY OSBOURNE SOLO ALBUMS

Date	Title/Tracks	Catalogue No.
September 12 1980	BLIZZARD OF OZZ — I Don't Know; Crazy Train; Goodbye To Romance; Dee; Suicide Solution; Mr. Crowley; No Bone Moves; Revelation (Mother Earth); Steal Away (The Night)	JET LP 234
October 30 1981	DIARY OF A MADMAN — Over The Mountain; Flying High Again; You Can't Kill Rock And Roll; Believer; Little Dolls; Tonight; S.A.T.O.; Diary Of A Madman	JET LP 237
November 1982	TALK OF THE DEVIL — Symptom Of The Universe; Snowblind; Black Sabbath; Fairies Wear Boots; War Pigs; The Wizard; N.I.B.; Sweet Leaf; Never Say Die; Sabbath Bloody Sabbath; Iron Man; Children Of The Grave; Paranoid. Recorded live at The Ritz, New York 26/27 September 1982. Featuring Brad Gillis (guitar), Rudio Sarzo (bass) and Tommy Aldridge (drums).	Jet DP 401 double LP
December 1983	BARK AT THE MOON — Rock'n'Roll Rebel; Bark At The Moon; You're No Different; Now You See It (Now You Don't); Forever; So Tired; Waiting For Darkness; Spiders. *American version has two different tracks **Lord And Lady** and **Slow Down** replacing Spiders and one other track. The title was changed to suit American sensibilities.	Epic EPC 25739

IMPORT ALBUMS

Title	Tracks	Catalogue No.
The Original Black Sabbath 1978	N.I.B.; War Pigs; Changes; Tomorrow's Dream	NEMS German import
Best Vibrations	Black Sabbath; The Wizard; Warning; Paranoid; War Pigs; Iron Man; Wicked World	NEMS ZNLNE 33116 Italian import
Star Gold	includes most tracks fro "We Sold Our Soul . . ." plus another track; 'Solitude'	NEMS German double import
Rock Legends	Back Street Kids; Rock'n'Roll Doctor; Dirty Women; Never Say Die; Shock Wave; Air Dance; Johnny Blade	Vertigo 8321 120
Starburst		double import

BLACK SABBATH TRACKS ON ROCK COMPILATION ALBUMS

Title	Track	Catalogue No.
Axe Attack Vol 2	Die Young	K-Tel
Heavy Metal	Mob Rules	
Radio Active	Paranoid	
Live And Heavy	Paranoid	NEMS NEL 6020
Heavy Rock	Die Young; Heaven And Hell	
Double Hard	Paranoid (live)	

BOOTLEG ALBUMS

Title	Tracks	Catalogue No. etc.
Death Riders/Their Satanic Majesties Return	War Pigs; Neon Knights; Heaven And Hell; N.I.B.; Iron Man; Die Young; Paranoid	Witch Records LSD-666-WRS80-3 Recorded on Aug. 17 1980 — U.S.A. stereo
Killing Yourself To Die	Supertzar; Symptom Of The Universe; Snowblind; War Pigs; Black Sabbath; Medley — Dirty Women, drum solo, Rock'n'Roll Doctor; Medley — guitar solo, improvisation; Electric Funeral, guitar solo, N.I.B.; Gypsy; Paranoid; Children Of The Grave	Stone Records 4 double album. Recorded on April 21 1977 — Sweden stereo
Doomsday Recitation	Same tracks as "Killing Yourself To Die"	Impossible Recordworks stereo
Grindlepol	Killing Yourself To Live; Hole In The Sky; Snowblind; Killing Yourself To Live (2); War Pigs; Children Of The Grave	TAKRL 1379. Recorded during 1975 U.S. tour
Love In Chicago	Sweet Leaf; Killing Yourself To Live; Tomorrow's Dream; Snowblind; Sabbra Cadabra; What To Do; Supernaut; Iron Man; Black Sabbath; Children Of The Grave; War Pigs; Paranoid	Berkeley 2049/2050. Recorded 1973 mono
The 1978 American Tour	Black Sabbath; Iron Man; Paranoid; Symptom Of The Universe; War Pigs; Gypsy; Children Of The Grave	6144 mono

Unorthodox	Snowblind; Black Sabbath; Iron Man; Paranoid; Killing Yourself To Live; Hole In The Sky; War Pigs		Impossible Recordworks IMP 1–29. Recorded at U.S. venues in 1975 and 1978 stereo
London Hammersmith Odeon	Supertzar; War Pigs; Neon Knights; N.I.B.; Children Of The Sea; Sweet Leaf; Lady Evil; Black Sabbath; Heaven And Hell; Iron Man; Die Young; Paranoid; Children Of The Grave		BMO 8101 A/B/C/D. Recorded Jan. 20 1981 double album stereo
Nuclear Poisoner	Neon Knights; N.I.B.; Children Of The Sea; Sweet Leaf; Black Sabbath; Heaven And Hell; Iron Man		Recorded in Japan in 1981

VIDEO TAPES

Recorded at the Hammersmith Odeon in 1978
Tracks: Supertzar; Symptom Of The Universe; War Pigs; Snowblind; Never Say Die; Black Sabbath; Dirty Women; Rock'n'Roll Doctor; Electric Funeral; Children Of The Grave; Paranoid

BOOTLEG TAPES

Title	Details		
Newcastle '78		California Jam '74 and Santa Monica '75	C-60
Italy '73			
Megaton Surprise	Hammersmith Odeon June 19 1978 C90	Lewisham Odeon	October '75 C-90
		Gaumont State Theatre, Kilburn	November 21 '75 C-90
Pittsburgh 17/9/78 and London January '77	C60	Cardiff Capitol Theatre	November 22 '75 C-90
Bristol Colston Hall	1975, C-120	Hammersmith Odeon	March 12 '77 C-90
Southampton		Hammersmith Odeon	March 13 '77
Germany 1970	C60 (the version of War Pigs on this tape has different lyrics)	Glasgow Apollo	May 18 1978 C-90
		Hammersmith Odeon	1978 C-90
		Manchester Apollo	May 23 1980 C-90
Paris 1971	C60	Hammersmith Odeon	January 20 '81 C-120
Greens Playhouse, Glasgow	March 1973 C-90	Newcastle City Hall	January 6 1982 C-90
		Hollywood Bowl	October '72 C-60